COOKED ORANGES

other books by the author

POETRY
Dawn Visions
Burnt Heart/Ode to the War Dead
This Body of Black Light Gone Through the Diamond
The Desert is the Only Way Out
The Chronicles of Akhira
Halley's Comet
Awake as Never Before
The Ramadan Sonnets
The Blind Beekeeper
Mars & Beyond
Laughing Buddha Weeping Sufi
Salt Prayers
Ramadan Sonnets (The Ecstatic Exchange revised edition)
Psalms for the Brokenhearted
I Imagine a Lion
Coattails of the Saint
Abdallah Jones and the Disappearing-Dust Caper
Love is a Letter Burning in a High Wind
The Flame of Transformation Turns to Light
Underwater Galaxies
The Music Space
Cooked Oranges

THEATER / THE FLOATING LOTUS MAGIC OPERA COMPANY
The Walls Are Running Blood
Bliss Apocalypse

THE FLOATING LOTUS MAGIC PUPPET THEATER
The Mystical Romance of Layla & Majnun
The Journey to Qalbiyya

COMPILATION OF QUOTES
Warrior Wisdom

PROSE
Zen Rock Gardening
The Little Book of Zen
Zen Wisdom

COOKED ORANGES

poems

July 23, 2004 – January 24, 2005

Daniel Abdal-Hayy Moore

The Ecstatic Exchange
2007
Philadelphia

Cooked Oranges
Copyright © 2007 Daniel Abdal-Hayy Moore
All rights reserved.
Printed in the United States of America

For quotes any longer than those for critical articles and reviews, contact:
The Ecstatic Exchange,
6470 Morris Park Road, Philadelphia, PA 19151-2403
email: abdalhayy@danielmoorepoetry.com

First Edition
ISBN: 978-0-6151-6308-6 (paper)
Published by *The Ecstatic Exchange*,
6470 Morris Park Road, Philadelphia, PA 19151-240

Cover and text design by Abdallateef Whiteman / www.ianwhiteman.com
Cover collage by the author
Back cover photograph by Malika Moore

DEDICATION

to
Shaykh ibn al-Habib
(and the continuation of the Habibiyya)
Shaykh Bawa Muhaiyaddeen,
all shuyukh of instruction and ma'arifa
and
Baji Tayyaba Khanum

*The earth is not bereft
of Light*

CONTENTS

A Note About the Title 8

1 No Sleep 11
2 Elemental Forces 12
3 Beginnings of Jokes Without Endings 14
4 From the Tag End of a Dream 16
5 Arrangements 17
6 The Cloak of the Saint 21
7 Come Sunday 24
8 Scattered Ramses 27
9 The Silver Knot 29
10 Grief 31
11 Moments After 34
12 Non-event 35
13 Song 39
14 Low Tide 41
15 Aesthetic 42
16 All of It 43
17 Mist 44
18 Tiny Thread 47
19 Rune 50
20 True Faces 52
21 Air Circulates Around the Great and Small 55
22 Marrakech en Marche 60
23 Gnomic Sentences 67
24 The Wingless Child 70
25 The Very Delicate Egyptian Glass Vial 72
26 Keeping it Simple 75
27 Royal Golden Lions 77
28 King Midas 20/20 79
29 Very Tiny Gazelles 81
30 Horse Knowledge 83

31 Angel Pranks 85
32 Terrible 89
33 Ramadan Rapture 92
34 The Poems I Want to Read 94
35 The Radiance of Day 99
36 The Road 101
37 The World's Bundle/November 3, 2004 103
38 The Dead 105
39 The Sleep Train 107
40 Tongue-tip to Tongue-tip 109
41 The Forest of Sleep 112
42 I Lay Back Down 113
43 A Vermin's Tale 115
44 The Dynasty of Durability 118
45 There's the Train That Stops 119
46 Alchemical Wedding 121
47 The Way of the World 123
48 Grace Descending 126
49 The Lion Who Wanted to Sing 128
50 More Sunlight Let Through 136
51 Direct Passage 138
52 There Was a Reply 141
53 A Short Shoe Saga 144
54 Doors 146
55 The Alchemist's Lesson 148
56 Line From a Dream Poem 151
57 Saga of the Sea Sponge 152
58 Why There are Stars 154
59 The Sleep of the Dead 156
60 But it is We 157
61 Poem Given in a Dream 159
62 Last Will & Testament 160
63 Poem that Puts into Perspective 163

A NOTE ABOUT THE TITLE

HONESTLY, I DON'T KNOW why *Cooked Oranges*. I know, it sounds like marmalade. It isn't meant to sound like marmalade.

This is the way it works for me: a title comes to me when I've ended the poems for one book and am about to begin another. The title almost always (I'm wracking my brain to recall an exception) comes first. The poems flow from it. Sometimes the title presents a kind of "theme," most notably in *Ramadan Sonnets*, *Mars & Beyond*, or *Laughing Buddha Weeping Sufi*, and the poems continue "exploring" that theme – often rather loosely, with many detours and sideline takeoffs – until the steam runs out, as it were, and the book has an ending. Then a new book begins. Usually fairly quickly, if not right away.

In this case, *Cooked Oranges* came to me right after the book, *Underwater Galaxies* (title from a Maximus line by Charles Olson), and the poems begin their orderly or disorderly arrival, usually in the middle of the night or at Dawn Prayer, either upon waking or afterwards, when the suds of consciousness are awash and light filters through. *Cooked Oranges* has less apparent meaning than most of my titles, and an almost Dada quality which I both like and wonder at. I could easily have changed the title by, say, taking the title from one of the poems in the collection and making it the "title poem." But I feel an obligation to my inspiration to keep the title as it came in all its naked resplendence… or else in its Thrift Shop tatteredness.

Poetic inspiration continues to be a mystery to me, but I am its deep advocate, and hold to its irrational and shady acreage like a greedy real estate developer gazing out over the possibilities (a ramshackle hut here, a barn there, a castle with a lake yonder…). Is it angels, djinn, my black cat curled at the bottom of my bed while I'm hot in composition mode? My "unconscious," "God Consciousness?" (my fervent prayer). I make no claims, I don't enter a trance state exactly, and these are not visual Technicolor visions, visitations (Ah William Blake, Ibn Farid, Rumi!) nor the reports of true dreams, though they are a kind of channeling, and I really am not now writing this note the one who writes the poems (when I'm not in composition mode, I mean *in the very act of writing*, I say I'm the poet's "earthly" representative, his front man, his PR man).

But I have a constant feeling that the sea of love Allah surrounds us with, with all its language-waves, thought-currents, and just general molecular sparkle, is feeding us in our tiny human pool bodies, and if we incline to listen and hearken, yes, *hearken* (nice old word) to its speech we might transcribe its sinewy lines on our "completely modern" material pages. And somehow we may partake of a portion of some of those higher and diviner inspirations however we define them, and I would wager that most poets of conviction, even more secular in bent, might say the same thing.

Each of the poems in my entire work from first to last comes in a similar fashion, and I have hammered a habit home to always carry my notebook with me, the way Beat bard Allen Ginsberg did, in a little shoulder pouch, in order to be there when the command comes to "*write!*" When a first line comes, it either has within it (as if softly pounding on a coffin lid from inside) the rest of the poem *en potentia*, or is only a one-line wonder, which may either become a one line poem (wonder or not) or be a dud, dead in the water, which I ignore (cross out, rip out of my notebook, though I am embarrassed to say there are very few).

Training oneself in the habit of attention is the key thing here, listening for that sometimes distant coffin-lid knock-knock-knocking, and be ready to stir oneself to active duty… letting the writing hand (no, not quite automatically, but almost) curve across the page like an arched and singing rainbow over parched fields.

So *Cooked Oranges*, whatever they may be. For the tasting (maybe marmalade isn't a bad idea after all). And may their channeled inspirations be… well, *inspirations*.

"Show me things as they are."

— TRADITION OF THE PROPHET MUHAMMAD,
(peace and blessings of Allah be upon him)

1   NO SLEEP

    Something in me doesn't want to sleep

    I might wake up in the rubble of Berlin
    or marooned on an island wearing shoes
    or after everyone has left the train as it
    chugs its desolation through the Alps

    Or the light has gone out of the world

    And the tea set for the saints in their crystalline robes
    has no place for me at either a side table or even
    way back in the shadows of the room where I might
    hear fragments of their conversation concerning

    the way light filters through the trees of Paradise in gradated
    rays each color of which each musical
    saturated color of which has a definite meaning in our
    various spectrums of solitude mostly abandoned by a sudden

    sweet Godly closeness

                                                           7/23

2 ELEMENTAL FORCES

The sun sets in a glass
and rises in a flute

The moon floats in an hourglass
and sheds its rays in a lamp

The daylight hangs in hammocks in the trees
or scrubs itself at one of those
outside showers at the beach

Night comes in on slender silver rollers
Night stands in the doorway bare-chested

Halos of light are sliced out of a neon tube
heads of light are placed within them at the
same moment and they both shine

Lit scallops on the ocean's breakers dip like spoons
dark roars inside big swells and hisses
on the shore

Lengths of time are stretched out on a brass table
that tarnishes at their touch

Tender kisses are turned into drenching downpours
lightning hang glides from a birch tree
thunder sits in a dish that breaks into twelve equal parts

Icicles form a phantom boat full of phantom men
whose dirge is caught in a net of isotopes

Light seeps out the edges in the letter to God
Who seals the flap with liquid rock
then sends it to Himself under a bridge of sighs
before the cascading cataract of our heartbeats
closes its eyes

I don't see any point in ending this
on anything but a high note

So the aurora borealis of our blood
hangs in shimmering fuchsia curtains

above a single bass note

across an Arctic breaking up into
hiccups of ice

clicking in billion-part harmony

to the glory of their Lord

3   BEGINNINGS OF JOKES WITHOUT
    ENDINGS

Three toads and an Episcopalian Minister were
walking down the road one day…

A bar went into a bar one night after
closing time…

The horse in its horse stall turned and looked its
trainer in the eye…

Seven hundred left-handed lawyers in shiny Saks 5th Avenue suits
walked right up to the edge of a cliff and one said to the other…

One house burned down with all its inhabitants in it
a second house burned down with all its inhabitants in it
a third house refused to burn…

A spaghetti noodle three miles long said to
the Italian chef who stood at an open pot…

A whale pod was resting just off the shore of
Newfoundland when a walrus swam by…

An icicle fell straight down from a roof
into the heart of the adulterous next door neighbor…

A group of blimps was floating across the
Venetian sunset one summer evening…

Michaelangelo looked up at the Sistine chapel one
morning and said to his assistant...

A chips dealer at Las Vegas died and went to
heaven and Saint Peter said to him...

After the cannibals ate the very fat and tasty missionaries and
were sitting around under a tree picking their teeth...

Adam told Eve to hush for the first time in his life
he could hear something slither through the grass...

A rock sat down in the middle of the road
and wiped its brow...

I began to write this knowing there'd be
no end in sight

                                                             7/26

4 FROM THE TAG END OF A DREAM

In our lifetime we'll see the invention
of clear ice cream

7/26

5   ARRANGEMENTS

I fell asleep near my 64th birthday thinking of my brother
ten years older than me wondering what
arrangements he's made for his
death and whether they're like those of our
parents who chose incineration and the awkward
scattering of ashes as I did with my mother's on a
windy California hilltop in the suburbs against a
grayish-blue day those flakes and charred bits
blustering across a slope into the trees and grasses
as if sowing impossible seeds for a ghostly harvest

And then thought of my own "arrangements" in that
as a Muslim I'll be washed and wrapped and
lowered in a parcel of earth for ultimate resurrection

And wonder at people's and even creatures' "arrangements"
over all
the woolly mammoth excavated hairy and nearly intact
having simply lain down or blown down to that position by some
mortal blow or wind or inner failure
a tusked continent dropped in its tracks
and our own strange arrangements century after
century of human history the various

elaborations of internment fanciful or divine brutal or
as delicate as loosing candles on the Ganges
in lily pad saucers

faint glimmerings flickering across the dark afloat on an
earthly element and quenched in the atmosphere

to reappear in a non-earthly element for
longer than their appearance lasted here

2

I think of grand gold carriages and their retinues
horses and riders all sacrificed for the great Khan
or the Peruvian mummies wrapped like packages and
slid into jars
or the Himalayan buzzard feasts of first the bodies themselves
then the chopped remains then the pulverized bones mixed with
barley or whatever to entice vulturely appetite

As we choose our way of the ultimate disposal of our own
physical forms which are so ever-presently here when
here at all and so

otherworldly *not* here once we're gone

The mouse in its hole dying in its sleep
or insects who turn to dust after their
exoskeleton stays put for days as the soft inner parts are
eaten by ants and the hard outer parts just disintegrate away completely
over time

Time itself who looks at us once on the way back from Timelessness
and smiles a real smile of victory over us
as we pass which we can take either as
gloating or benignity depending on the
tempers of our hearts before these

final "arrangements" are indelibly put into place

3

I feel my bodily form its
warmth and arms and legs

its pulse pulsating like a controlled tremor
like an undercurrent so strong I can

go to sleep on it and drift to a far planet
and wake up on it and it's still dependably there
though it's not my own but was given me at birth
and is I think the surf I'll go out again on
in death

The livingmost clench of soul-life who loves the paradisiacal banquet
seeking its odors and tastes and longing for its
music if it's perceived too far away in a distant forest grove
for immediate tuning

The throb that pushes the pen as I write this and
sees these words forming under its eyes

The throb that connects us all no matter what
high altitude or lower depth we may inhabit on earth

and on whose noble choir of soundlessness

we are sustained once all this mortality is shut to us
forever with no chance of reentry although

some might interpret the incredibly wheeling and rotating
throb of life to mean the reappearance of our
entity in either more elegant or

inelegant garb than our present one

trailing streamers from one world into the next
our loud voices hushed and our cries

turned into song at last

7/26

6 THE CLOAK OF THE SAINT

I

The cloak of the saint was filled with roses

The cloak of the saint rose above the city

The cloak of the saint was thrown over the back of a chair
it slowly filled with a human form
it was filled with the sound of wind

It floated down the mountainside
sheep it passed turned golden

Rocks glowed in its light as it flowed across their surfaces

It sat at the table of the poor and broke bread

It spoke to a lone man on a rooftop or mountaintop
a lone woman standing by a stream or sink
a child singing to himself in the bath
a child playing by herself in a corner filled with bric-a-brac

Or at sea in a lifeboat where a single sailor lies dying
or a young scholar weeping for joy in a lamplit mosque in the snow

Or over the silent morning where the birds are
just now waking up in the trees

2

The saint's cloak is not made of threads interwoven
but of silences between words and then
words like pearls lifted and suspended in the air between silences

The saint's cloak covers windows and doors
our entrances and exits and all the indecisive or decisive
moments in between

Along rolling green hillsides just as the sun first hits them at dawn
and as the sun pulls its light into darkness at dusk
the cloak unfurls and is not light of sun nor dark of night
and maybe it's closer to starlight in its distant and elegant splendor
though it's as near as the web of skin between
forefinger and thumb or the
raw inner flesh of our eyelids in a biting wind
or in a corridor of mirrors when an eyelash is
caught in them

Or alone on a beach where the cloak rises and
falls with the lull of waves and the
sound of a bell buoy ringing invisibly in the mist

If it were spread out against the sky its
words could be read more easily

Its parchment its scroll-like unrolling across the entire
length and breadth of our lives in its impeccable grammar
its perfect punctuation its start of sentence and
single *point final*

The saint's cloak drifting neither upward nor downward
but drifting all the same

From one end of us to the other

Through whose fabric towers of ice arise

The living tremor of an uncommon surrender

                                                  7/27-28

7   COME SUNDAY

Come Sunday the cogs and wheels that run things
will have identified themselves
a hat will be a hat not a *"skull-covering dome"* or
"that which keeps the stars out"

It's not too farfetched to say that come Sunday
windows will no longer be just transparent
interruptions in walls
but actual events in and of themselves with
notable full-color consciousnesses on either side
one looking out from within and one looking
in from without

The river of light that runs through everything will
sparkle like the Milky Way and the sky-stretch overhead by
day or night will be more than a *"celestial portal"*
or *"inverted bowl"* (and if it is
then does that make us merely the tumbled-out contents?)
or simply an endless highway of pinpointed sky
pulled taut over the endless highway that runs across Texas

All these things come Sunday will be a cause for
celebration a pause between humdrum and ho-hum
a sudden seltzer in otherwise flat cola

Suddenly and as if without warning
the veriest walkalong caterpillar will be a
many-legged barefoot fuzzy gentleman or
gentlewoman going toward
his or her ultimate transformation splendiferously
radiant and fluttery as
light itself

The landscape will be a garden tended by full-fledged gardener angels
from whose water-can spouts (ourselves) the most
glorious rainbowy sprays shoot forth in thirst-slaking drops

And each step on earth will ring bells since the
known destination that we take in whatever direction
is God's personal doorway entrance into His
Field of Divine Endeavors His Most Agreeable Convocation His
Promised Reciprocation to our most humble heartbeats and
most perfect opinions of Him in His both visibly and
invisibly multifaceted perfections

Not Utopia as such but an eye-cleansing starting with a
cardiac squeegee that insures no
flyspeck gets in the way that would blot out the
world
no gnat-splotch disfigure the sublime elegance that is
the reality of each moment we're alive

And whose radiant glories accompany us beyond whatever
abject or distinguished grave is reserved for us in earth's antechambers
to which we go clear-eyed and clear-headed
singing a soldier's tune of subliminal halleluiahs
and audible appreciative melismas those
full-throated soarings of notes gliding from
low to high and from high to low or from high to yet higher

whose time-signature is the invincible heart metronome of each
moment from most deeply within us

The same place of utter actual silence that serves as a
starting gate for sleek white horses fleeter than the wind
and illuminating nuclear reactions all the way
from our breaths to the universe's outermost edge

which is the intangible but apprehensible
edge of each epiphany whose profile will show itself

at last come Sunday and every day
thereafter dear God

come Sunday
in full sunlight

and every day
dear God

thereafter

7/30/04
(64th birthday)

8 SCATTERED RAMSES

Scattered Ramses petrified mummy
Gathered himself from various relic drawers

Put his gaudy jewelry on
Sat in a chair with crook and ankh

Tried to look fierce but only looked dead
Half his wrappings coming off

Smiled the rictus smile of a skull
Couldn't command quite the same response

No one bowed or groveled chattering
No one fanned him with a papyrus fan

He waited for days in the dark museum
No wife clamped his anklet on

No one served him royal supper
Though he couldn't really chew

No one slew some dark-skinned captives
No one hauled heavy pyramid stones

No one in fact did anything at all
Poor Ramses sat there all alone

Deader than a doornail to everyone's consciousness
Except his own which to him was legion

Finally something fell in a corner
Clattered to the floor a sword or broom handle

Now he felt strong again now he felt powerful
Now he felt vindicated for all his cruelty

Someone was showing the proper respect
There in the dark of the old museum

Someone deferred to his awesome grandeur
Sitting on a deck chair all bones no skin

A broom handle athwart the parquet floor
The head of the broom flat down in his direction

Finally happy in the dark antiquities wing
Someone showed him the deference he deserved

8/1

9 THE SILVER KNOT

A slip of the silver knot
and all would be lost or saved
steadfastly tied to shore or
hanged from the gallows

I once saw a silver knot
behind a sacrificial bull's right ear
I asked my father what it meant
he shushed me faster than sunlight

A silver knot sits on a bedside table
in a velvet box encrusted with diamonds
the Marquise lays back on silken cushions
in a corner a violist plays *Liebenstraum*

The silver ends drawn through each other
in a looping knot as tight as moonlight
frayed at the ends with frail silver wires
a lethal combination of beauty and power

The silver knot lifted to the head of a horse
where a victorious general sits in his braid
he accepts the knot and the official surrender
one side cheers while the other side mourns

It floats in the air as if made of gossamer
a knot of light somehow optically tied
an alchemist stands back with his smashed alembic
covers his eyes against the sudden glare

"With this knot you are wed to mountains and streams
the air of night and the rocks of winter
cascades of summer to walk in peace
the way these silver strands are tied together"

The knot was thought to be a curse to some
to others a blessing especially the cautious
but Solveg wore it proudly on his tunic
as he surveyed the tundra like an open sea

Laughing she pulled at the silver knot
and a strand slid loose and the knot undid
and a single string lay limp before her
to the horror of her suitor the notorious pirate

Tall and bloody Bertram the One-Eyed
who was captured as his boat tied to shore
and hanged on the gallows the very next day
in a plaza whose name was *Nudo de Plata*

8/4

10 GRIEF

> *Grief is better than happiness, because in grief a person draws close to God. Your wings open. A tent is set up in the desert where God can visit you.*
>
> — BAHAUDDIN, FATHER OF MEVLANA RUMI

The wind is full of sand that walks with you
wherever you go

Intellectually windows are being soaped over and rooms
boarded up and the garden left
untended

Storks avoid the broken chimney pots

The nights are endless and the days pour into them
like grain down a sharp incline

Distant voices are as close as we can get to
the party whose purpose is obscure and whose
laughter seems inappropriate

Windows are being soaped over and shades drawn
and rooms left unentered except by the
innocent green moss of silent fungus

But in a remote area where the wind seems to originate
and the night seems almost varnished
a greenish yellowish glow begins to shine inside the
outpost where we've gone to be so alone it's as if
no one's ever been born on earth but ourselves

And a trail of ants attracts our attention
and time seems to stop moving horizontally and
starts climbing vertically and a
hand on the back of our neck and under the
root of our heart brings a welcome chill
out of the blue

God says we're never late to our appointment

He brings things into play even when we're
gazing elsewhere

Even the distant blue on the horizon of
racing steeds or blown debris is for our benefit

The tent of our refuge fills with light but not
suddenly

more glow by glow

Two shabbily dressed clowns fail to amuse us first
and the golden lady who threatens us with her
torch of goodness also leaves the precincts
unscorched in spite of her insouciance

God says you don't even begin to know how many
hoops have been jumped through on our behalf
and the fact that daybreak comes at all
is the result of a Titanic effort

though by Allah each
part of the machinery of its uprising falls
effortlessly into place

with no stone left unturned

and no antenna left untwitched

with His

subtlest communication

                                                       8/7

11 MOMENTS AFTER

A wild elephant sits down after its rampage
and dusts its brow with dirt

The dust settles after the building's collapsed to the
ground with everyone inside it
little flakes in universes of their own twirling and
tumbling through the air as if humming to themselves

After initial spews of disgorging flame the lava flow slides
cobra-like singing silently to itself down the hillside into the
valley below with only the crackle and pop of
burnt trees rooftops stalled automobiles
and whatever else is in its way

After the volcanic shout that cleaves the air
the room becomes silent more silent than our
honoring of the dead though not as silent as
the dead themselves

Menace replacing chitchat tension replacing gossip
expectation as wide as space itself replacing
the blithe sense of immortality that usually
accompanies all we do

8/12

12 NON-EVENT

Any event you can conceive of is not *The Event*

Though the snowfall you see falling is simply snow falling

I say this in the heat of summer that soaks our nightshirts

If we move so much as a micrometer the entire universe
shifts its feet like a restless horse

Even uttermost stillness in the eye of God is erratic vibration

His stillness outweighs the entire elegance of our
seemingly static cosmic state as it
swings all its galaxies wide of His central pivot

I say this at the side of my bed at 8:30 AM to the
sound and breeze-blast of a tall standing fan
oscillating the air around me
while my heart oscillates deep within me

A slow scarlet squiggle with golden sheen
takes place in a far off space somewhere like an airborne ribbon
that calligraphs *The Indecipherable*
surrounded by the blackness of night
in broad daylight

God the Generous
God the Hearer and Seer
how do I know You are here
except by the uninterrupted generosity of
Your Hearing and Seeing?

A small bubble is all we are
though we float happily in His abyss
reflecting various sharp-focus aurora borealises
off our surfaces as well as
other ecstatically bursting lights

I say this with my chin in my left palm and
left elbow on this open notebook as my right hand
scribbles these lines and my right foot
pains me with a strange attack of
non-gluttonous gout

Left to our own devices with all the impingements of
action or inaction
all the lifelong soul sources of our eagerness or reticence
would we fall into a deeper sleep or
awaken as never before?

I see the judge's chin by peering up over the front of his podium
who for a face has all the planets and their
circulating pockmarked moons

If we skip any of the important stages out of laziness we might
find ourselves stranded beyond the confluence of sacred rivers
unable to cross except by
death barge whose occupants sing in a
harmony so close as to be inaudible
though great black birds dip their wings as they glide above
on their way to Glory

I say this listening to the water pipes upstairs
shutting off with a jerk that reverberates throughout
the house

The heartbeat knows its own world with a
rhythm that speaks in extended sentences of the
origin and end of all things
the perpendicular epic to this daily world
we see we think and touch

If we sit long enough all the events that
bedevil us will fall away
and the empty warehouse awaiting
further orders will present itself out of blue mist
and not long afterward new backdrops and props
will roll in on perfect schedule ready for the
next drama to unfold

English sparrows land on branches out the window
in syncopated flocks
then fly off again in fluttering sheets of separate stars like
black sparks
heading for the far trees

I say this bending down as close as possible
to listen to this poem
as it gurgles over glistening rocks

I had no idea it would come to this

The sweetness of death is that it
encloses us again in a soft womb

God bless us in the purity of our search

8/13

13 SONG

If arrival in God's precincts were possible through song
we'd be in the company of crickets and canaries

oval after oval lifting the circumference of the globe
bluer than the turquoise at the bottom of the Caspian or

Mediterranean seas (if that's where it comes from)
more silvery than the silence of undersea leviathans in

quest of mammalian solitude by a coral reef or deep sea vent

If song could bring us closer to His blessing's coliseum
arm in arm with those who've preceded us in choirs

reaching notes no one's ever heard before like
color-streaks at sunset over deserts so remote only

appreciative lizards and prairie dogs see them
and happily nuzzle into the sand at night for warmth

having witnessed visual song in its unscrolled
splendor across the sky

If notes of wonder could bring us right up to the Holy One's breath
until we're not breathing on our own any more

with none of our own physical sustaining but only His
Benevolent aspirations and respirations seating us on cloud armchairs

and placing before us vapor tables set with ambrosia made of
pure song whole antelope herds gallop through each one of

them now singing with ants ascending grass blades
and gnats who've taken on the most

difficult melodies to prove that being minute in this
dark world doesn't matter

as long as we dare to sing and put all our
heart's hopes (one note at a time

to stretch the melody ever higher and
more openly oxygenated than space itself)

on song

8/14

14 LOW TIDE

"I can't see the horizon and its gargantuan sunset
due to strange spindle-like towers popped up across
the horizon"

Nothing can really be said to emanate from ourselves
to allay our sense of failure when time's tide rises
again between the short intervals of a possible sense of worthiness

Then the tide goes out and we're the empty beach and
God is the pounding ocean and a brilliant
sky full of white clouds

Call us back to Your center to tighten to a
spiritual tautness the very human
doggedness of our condition

By now the expositions of celestial eidolons should be
falling outward through my open heart
with no sense of mortal confinement

Little children and actual fawns should be
taking from Your largess
through these eyes and fingertips

my tongue alight with Your language

8/18

15 AESTHETIC

Poetry is what can't be said
any other way

Verse is thoughts searching for poetry

                                                            8/23

16 ALL OF IT

It can't be coaxed
the wind
to go thinly into a tiny chamber
except by Allah

Light
unless it is pushed ahead
by invisible forces
swifter than anything
remains in the dark

The captain
atilt on the high seas
unless he turn by Allah's bright stars
can't steer to safety

By Allah alone
these things and centipedes
fluttering along a branch
in a hurry or dreamy nights
on a bridge overlooking
moonlight

reflect in the face
like the first cause

Whose Face kept in shadow
unless Allah illumine it

opens this day
for us

8/23

17 MIST

The call you hear over the tops of the trees
may be coming from the bottom of your throat

The keys you hear jangling in the pocket of the distance
may already be opening an unsuspected way
before you

Laughter turning to sobs and back again to laughter
may be the beginning of a new song sung by a
character from the opera the blocked composer
suddenly composes and light floods his room

Three in the morning struck three times on the town clock
clanging its heavy bells may be the ushering in of a
silence so profound the rest of the morning
floats across it like gliding skaters in the
dead of winter

Your fortunes rise and fall before your eyes your
hopes lift and drop away leaving you exhausted from the
greyhound races of your emotions those sleek and
nervous runners bred too high-strung and too
delicately temperamental shying at the slightest sound
though once in a racing lane sure to win the competition

You've saved your life for the entrance music you imagine
will be played when you finally decide to put it
down not as down payment but as *Paid In Full*

every morsel and breath of you expended in the effort
not realizing *that's* the music you've been waiting for
all along

The heads of gazelle can be seen bobbing above the hedges

The shadows of eagles can be seen skimming the yellow
valleys and silvery streams

You take to the air with the same solemnity

You leap across open meadows with the same agility

But your eagle's voice and gazelle-like eyes and buoyancy
are nothing without a whale's deep thought and musicality
and the lion's noble silhouette on a sunset mountaintop insouciantly
yawning as the sun descends

It's not too late to stop consulting your watch for every move
it's early yet for the revelry to take its toll once your
eyes open on the actual saintliness of each
one of us in the same room and part of the
same conversation

Only then will your heart be served to you on the
platter you deserve and only then will your
absence be realized as having greater weight than your
presence

The sound of whispers along the midnight cobblestones

The message for your ears only by the blind youth with the
luminous face who stands by your door
as you enter transformed by the night mist into
intelligent mist yourself dispersing melodiously in the

gradual goldish mistlessness of dawn

8/24

18 TINY THREAD

A planetoid was about to be born in
some fairly distant galaxy from ours
invisible to our eyes due to stellar interference or
existing just beyond an obstructive lip of space-time curve
or sheer distance past every known patch of stars

and its mother star its solar womb was enduring all the
mysterious explosive cyclotronic gas-bang convulsive
combustions such procedures entail much as

ours when our mothers are about to give birth though we may be
ultimately less chunky after all even so

there's a mortal similarity to our own molecular
individuation in space our coming-to-birth in this world rather than
maintaining immateriality as our lifestyle eternally
remaining always out-of-view and at one entirely with
the Unseen in simple splendor rotating among its motionless
or torrential machinations previous to all
tangible existence wherever in our universe it might
take place presided over by The Guide of all the worlds
Who brings to birth and annihilates with compassionate aplomb

And this planetoid scrunched itself closer and more
protectively to its mother's molten core as if to
say it didn't want to go didn't want
expulsion from that Garden Paradise into the

tragic vicissitudes of space and finite
deteriorations of time

It wanted to remain forever at one with its
literal mother ship and moon around with
blinkless eyes gazing out thoughtfully at the
flare-ups and fiery displays and flashes-in-the-pan
fireworks in lugubrious slow motion that go on every
nanosecond in outer and inner space itself in an
inner place that had no part yet of space in that it
didn't yet independently exist as we do with all our
cleverness of mobilized hands and feet and motorized mischief
nosing around in snoopy corners of the universe in all our
endless curious or breathless quests

It longed to avoid a lifespan and just stay
atomically pure and undifferentiated

But the Decree was out the die was cast
and after explosion after explosion with true
astral regurgitations and labor pains too seismic to
recount our little planetoid spewed out intact into
space and began its lively orbit as well as its own
particular rotation around its infantile axis

and ice formed and rocks cracked and crevices opened and
angels sang and great cosmic chords sounded heard by
every shivering atom of existence however far or near in our own
mortal beings each spark registering even though deeply
unbeknownst to us

as we open our mouths with their glistening tongues and
glittering teeth to

speak or sing of

anything

Tiny thread in the weave without which
the whole would come unwoven

8/26

19 RUNE

Who stole my breath and
then stole me

Who hung my pelt
in the linden tree

Who left for dead
one of three

I took my armor
and set out to sea

Who everywhere was
there with me

Water as far
as the eye can see

There shall be no ending

Let them ignore
their ability

Cassandra could not speak
more truthfully

I am lost in the stars
like atomic debris

Take what you can
is my heartfelt plea

Forget the
monumentality

There is only beginning

8/27

20 TRUE FACES

The butcher conceals wings under his wraparound apron

The policeman is secretly psychic and can
solve all the cases

The jeweler plucks diamonds out of his mouth
when no one's looking

The dancer levitates alone in front of the practice room
mirror while slowly pirouetting with long
arms upraised

These silent phenomena these invisible heroes of the Miraculous

The surgeon with actual laser eyes who waits a little
when the others blink to look deeply into the
opened patient to the source

The nurse with divinely guided ears who hears
the cry inside the cry and the moan inside the
silent sufferers and the voice of the comatose
reciting its detailed litany and singing its
circumscribed dreams

Nothing is as it seems

The old crossing guard with the big bosoms and thick
glasses who whispers rosy destinies in eight-year-olds'
ears often without them noticing until
twenty years later one morning at breakfast

The florist who lives in visionary anticipation
sending bouquets to bashful lovers or the
recently bereaved signing their cards with
perfect appropriate signatures

The railroad engineer who entertains angels in the
locomotive cabin on those long nights in blinding blizzards
who tell him when to accelerate around curves

The Chinese shoemaker whose ancestors bring him the
next perfectly cut piece of leather or silk to sew in the
middle of the night for the next morning's
urgent commissions

The abyss opens up in a split second and
releases its evil denizens into the air
The muttering grandmother in the print housedress
gives them a withering glance that
dissolves their wicked intentions forever

The old black gardener in dust overalls who
talks to birds and listens to their sagas and
weeps tears at their aerial travails

This list only indicates a texture often overlooked in God's
impeccable creation

The light inside the listener that sheds on crystal
caverns where the true tablets lie in heaps
each face a decipherable text that tells our most
secret desires and the cures of the deepest
maladies of our deliverance

those individual afflictions which are
each of our safe passages to Paradise once we've

taken each one by the reins and ridden it in

8/28

21 AIR CIRCULATES AROUND THE GREAT AND SMALL

Air circulates around the great and small

On a high mountaintop in a fortified stronghold
the magi of Astrotropolis pull their thick woolen robes
around them and gaze at the far-off clouds
looking for signs

But the sign comes to them in the form of a tiny spider
who creeps carefully from a crack in the stones
and drops on its thread from the wooden-beamed ceiling
onto the head of Thetis of Thessalonia who scowls and
scratches
nearly annihilating our eight-legged hero who brings
God's news in an undecipherable language except to
advanced magi alone among tumultuous clouds
one hand on ancient texts the other raised in the air
forefinger lifted in the flickering candlelight

Our spider leaps and sidles down and lands on the flagstone floor
and climbs the table leg and finds the ancient text in question
and starts his web across the salient page
and sits in the corner and waits for
Ammon Celestialis to glance at the page and its
silken highlighting

It helps that a slanting sunbeam just so happens to
slide across the page from a high window and
illuminate both gossamer and passage at once

"Break rock with gentleness

Bring the heart to high waters to wash it

Let no dog die of thirst in your territories

Laugh at sadness weep at gifts

You shall not be left alone for long"

That little spider so cunningly crouched in her corner
and the mage's eyebrows looked like they'd caught fire as his
two black-as-coal eyes landed on those
volatile words as the wind blew out the tapers and he
recited them to the others sitting silent
in the dark

2

"Break rock with gentleness" he intoned in the
draughty dark

The others hummed in unison and a slow
glimmer began to take place somewhere in the
indefinite air

*"That you not harden it further by your
intense aggression but find instead its
weak point and that through gentleness"*

"I sing to my sorrows" one said
"and harmonize my perplexities"

*"I take a hammer to fasten boards
but for rock embraces and soft entreaties
and they crumble"*

*"The ocean is most forceful by its incessant soft beating
on the shore and only rarely lurches back and
unleashes its full fury"*

3

*"Bring the heart to high waters to wash it
in crystalline goblets at a cascade's crest*

*up from murk bring it up from the
weight of chains and previous detours*

*such a fist-sized entity holds the light of the
universe no other entity can hold with such
equanimity"*

And the magi hum together as if the
Potala in Lhasa were being reconsecrated
up its alleyways and lofty cloud chambers its

yak butter soot-darkened halls and sacred
corridors opened again for sacred use

Their own hearts humming now in closer proximity to
each other and each other thing of heart alive now in the
world inside apparent heartlessness

4

"Let no dog die of thirst in your territories

Several pickles short of a Dutch summer

Bronze the lesser metal and gold the head honcho

There's always a brilliant physicist crouching under the
lab table
whose name is Herman or Bridgett and who is
dangerously close to the Unified Theory of Everything including
the eyelash peskily detached and floating inside your
lower eyelid"

5

Laugh at sadness weep at gifts
you shall not be left alone for long

The breath our true companion lifts
the entire world on bands of song

Horse-drawn buggies through streets by day
and what we know but will not say

And at each turning in the road we see
streaks of red that blast the sky

9/8

22 MARRAKECH EN MARCHE

1

The golden dome in the distance shines like the
corolla of a sunflower toward which

all the cattle graze hoping for a glimpse of its light
each hoofbeat tapping out the

language of its beefy sorrow
each lowing with a voice seemingly out of nowhere

that suddenly makes of nowhere a
definite place

2

Only Allah is not *nowhere*
as well as not *where*

whereas all else but Allah is either
where or *nowhere here* or *there*

what or *whatnot*
how or *how in the world*

in or *not of this world*
of or *from* this world

or even *not* from this world
nor the next

and we are left
with our hearts alone

to know this

Who knows only Himself

3

I sat next to an alcoholic on the airplane
and found myself getting judgmental

I don't know the broken prairies the slammed doors
the tragic marriages or the DNA code
hammering out its insistent melody on the same
low melancholic piano

He had that blotch-faced beaten look
and a kind of aristocratic angry dignity either
English or French with stories to tell no doubt
when the rage overtakes him

going home to Essouira

4

Death has its own cloak it throws around us

I thought of a man I knew who flew from
South Africa to London and slept the whole way
and when he got up keeled over and died

Just like this airplane full of light and laughing chatter
bleached white sky out the window
growl under us of motor grinding us through the air

And I can't conceive of it or me disappearing in death
out the leveraged corridor
gone forever from it

it also gone forever

5

A scaly dragon turned out to be
docile after all
and two swans absolutely lethal

A water buffalo chatted with its
master on the road
pop goes the weasel

A parrot did its repertoire
faster than a blink
a butterfly wished it were back
at caterpillar brink

A gnat had visions of dimensional grandeur
until the wind blew it into the abyss
of a dog's mouth door
who sealed it with a
wag of its tail

faster than a semaphore
happier than a flail

6

*"Our lives are occasional false respites from a general
sense of unworthiness"*
says the haggard washerwoman scrubbing out
impossible stains

The dray horse pulling a tourist carriage
through the terra cotta lanes of Marrakech

the fly who tries to land on the best spot
but never quite finds it

the water spray doing its best to irrigate the
lavish hotel lawn for the delight of its guests

the sky itself between bouts of rain or
bouts of sunshine

words themselves between chitchat and
absolute silence

7

*"How dare you pull your pen across a page again
when a blind white goat in a green field chomps the grass
and a child doesn't know why*

*Or a man has his head in a bucket and his legs in a
bear trap in the middle of summer at a
luxurious resort on the Mediterranean*

*Why the locomotive puffs and chugs its way uphill
carrying its passengers to disaster and out again*

*Or the ice caps are melting at a worrisome rate
especially for the mountain villages below"*

said the very small ant to me before continuing
on its way

I have no other answer but this broken song

8

World travel isn't so much traveling the world
as weaning oneself *from* it

9

All British Air passenger seats have television screens

All passengers in the passenger seats have heart screens

The television screens play movies and news and the map of our
present location with a little white airplane
somewhere over the Atlantic

The heart screens play everything that exists in the universe
brought into focus with selected particulars by everyone's allotted
soul toils and soul imprints and the subtle and less
subtle pictographs of each one's gifts

The television screens only about 3½ x 5 inches in diameter contain
the violent thousands of battle on the beach at Troy or an
English sitcom with its canned laughter and
high-pitched giggles

The heart screens contain all that is Allah and
nothing that is other-than-Allah if we but knew

"Kill Bill" is playing on a screen in front of me
"Harry Potter" on a screen to my right

God is pouring ambrosial sweetness on a white-haired
man's heart who's returning from his daughter's funeral
while callisthenic details and memories of
Marrakech sunbathing are flowing together in a
blond girl's heart as she presses her boyfriend's hand
through a few air pocket bumps

though behind those scenes of earthly delight
God's bright snow is also falling

The seat screens turn off with one touch of the finger
the heart screens become only more vast

with time and death and
go on forever

9/10-9/15 (Marrakech, Morocco)

23 GNOMIC SENTENCES

The sweetness of the bitter pill
the ascent of the small step

The total silence of too much speaking
the eyeful that becomes blind

The touch that becomes a full embrace
the downfall that becomes its own rise

See the sun in a mirror before
shielding your eyes from its rays

See the heart's mirror down in your depths
turning dragons into doves

The laughter that is crueler than a scythe
the scimitar more soothing than comforting words

In some extremes have become the norm
for some the norm drives them to extremes

Kiss the stone in the corner of the house
and pass it by

The center never leaves its pivotal location
the edges never cease to be peripheral

A drop of honey on a sheet of glass
is an amber metropolis

An ant is a cosmos on six legs
holding a leaf

Hold to true notions and look death
straight in the face

Though the hair on the back of your hands
stand up and your throat parch

The gallows looks like a distant threat
for everyone else

Some eloquent words have escaped the lips
of those about to be hanged

Down has never been up
though it leads to the wheel

Each turn of the wheel by day or night
climbs the difficult mountain

Far is near for those who've just
returned from a journey

Lean close to the voyager who's
passed through the Pleiades

The sighs of these journeyers are worth
more than the sacred texts

Look and see if you're too much there
to partake of their nothingness

The ocean hides her inhabitants
with ferocious modesty

On earth the ocean is the air we breathe
and God is the whale surveying us with serene eyes

Let go of holding on
and holding on will let go of you

The flight to another planet
brings us back to earth with a jolt

A bolt of light is enough
to see a moment of space

God's Light is enough to fill each breath
with His Face

9/16

24 THE WINGLESS CHILD

The wingless child looked up and the sky
was filled with circling lights as if its

gears and belts were suddenly visible and the
stars were simply stationary sparks thrown

out by its machinery
and distant spaces

The light years between bodies were shrunk to
approachable timetables and the backs of other

universes were also visible with their own peculiar

angularities or amorphous shapes of heavier-than-
iron in sheet shapes or shapes of light around which

slowly circulating angel masses were moving
and the child's eyes became beacons and his

heart a city of spires and his body also became
as if feathers were ascending through glycerin

calling out to all the creatures of creation
names as first articulated in Adam's primal vocabulary

every atom eloquent in chains and loops in
leapfrog acrobatics incandescently loquacious

and interlinked in their actual phosphorescent grammar
as spoken by each thought or thing

            9/20

25 THE VERY DELICATE EGYPTIAN GLASS VIAL

I

The very delicate Egyptian glass vial all
striated spirals of gray blue and cobalt silver

contains a bit of sand which is a whole desert
a bit of moisture which is every ocean known
plus a few unknown
and a space of air that is all space and air inhaled by
every inhabitant of every planetary orb habitable in the
vast skies beneath and above us and all

around us like folds of great starry cloaks once
surrounding and lying so lightly on
the shoulders of the most saintly in
knowledge and most penetrating of insight

whose shadow cast on this revolving earth would in
fact not cover the smallest gnat and yet nearly
blots out the sun with its intenser illumination

I send out these long ribbons in hopes they'll somehow
outline a light like neon tubing that advertises the most
divine ice cream in town

I try to sit back and let minglings of light and
dark do all the work the way
a dark barn might give birth to a halo'd
wobbly foal or a

deep wood conceal a lame deer in its motherly dark

Yet everything's contained in everything else
and everything's nothing at last just as it was at
first but only an enticing fiction that
dazzles our senses with its jangling apocalyptic jewelry

knowing we will have to be brave at least once in our lifetimes
though we must be brave each moment
facing death with each out-breath that could

extend itself infinitely and suddenly be
our very last

knowing that at the end of it just beyond its silvery edge

God's Compassionate Face
awaits us

2

Every peak has its abyss
every abyss its high point

Each owl its prey imprinted in its eyes
each mouse an owl-god staring from its altar branch

Each night growls to itself in its sleep
though lions sleep by day and by night are as
restless and vigilant as ghosts

The roundest orb has a nicked notch it catches on
the smoothest curve has a fixed stopping point that locks

Every clock eventually runs down and space takes over
every space between things rests in this world but wakes on
Judgment Day like everybody else

Judgment Day comes and goes and leaves us tremblingly lame
with Olympic strength enough to leap the deepest length
across the highest abyss in endless hope

After silence comes abrupt quiet then
sudden hush then a long sensation of
motionlessness as if the earth were
rotating backwards
then a hiss only ants are aware of
but keep the knowledge to themselves and
each other along lines miles long they pass the
song along

Each car wreck has its resurrection

Each casualty its requiem

The nurse who looks after sick children
is already in heaven

9/22

26 KEEPING IT SIMPLE

"Keep it simple" sang the unicorn
as it was shown the door

The Dodo bird that couldn't fly
the Passenger Pigeon that could

And of course the cuddly dinosaur
in tar or out
casting a last nostalgic look with its
beady eye as it too
goes under

The Woolly Mammoth in spite of its
size that matters or its great curved
tusks that ultimately didn't

The bygones of all these certainly
will be bygones along with
the rest of us

A single sliver in the light a
single splinter of light in the dark

Our souls though larger than lunar
reflecting the sun
leap from the abyss of loss into
perfect day

pulling combs of starshine through
nonexistent hair

Looking at the true simplicity of
somethingness past all materiality

God's Light looking at God's Light at last
no shadows cast but his Name
in sheer reverberation and purest repetition

I'm last but not lost
and least of all

longing to be lost
in His Everlastingness

9/24

27 ROYAL GOLDEN LIONS

Royal golden lions roaming the Serengeti
serve to remind us that the best meals may not be ones
served on a plate

Dust clouds over the Great Plains just above
stampeding buffalo are signs that stasis has its
place on this earth but rarely generates such
spectacular billowing speech balloons as these whose
language is an awed silence and the
beating of hooves

The sky above the sloping backs of elephants in herds
slowly making their way to greener pastures to satisfy their
hungry tonnage and the shy twinkle in their tiny elephant eyes
has an even vaster breadth than their
lumbering bulk and seems to almost cloak their
nobility with the great blue
cloud-highlighted ermines they deserve

Oh God Who's fashioner and refiner of souls
filling us with a feathery breath in an
airy script whose words we can almost read in a
literal way but whose meaning expands past
the mechanics of such earthly grammar

each transcendent thing nestled in each worldly manifestation
in such a way really that even in the

dark there are blazing eyes of love that see us and
are drawn to each detail as a lover is to his
beloved's most secret attributes

The backs of our hands nestle against invisible thighs
our heartbeats are throbbing against a chest lying back
on a green hillside

Our evanescent spirits listening to all this with
wide open wonder as each gnat
greets another on its way by an almost
imperceptible buzzing of translucent wings

And we are their insoluble witnesses

Our attention the vertical air current rippling through the
daylight

and the single horizontal light beam that awakens the most
somnolent horizon

9/27

28 KING MIDAS 20/20

King Midas touched one more thing
just to make sure it was happening

Then a pin that suddenly dazzled with starlight and
became gold

A wooden button with its puny threads now
glittering and solid and bound with golden fibers
to the cloth of his coat

Now he dared the coat itself and found himself
encased in soft armor
all its buttons gleaming and the pockets solid shut
and the arms heavy

King Midas watched a ladybug land nearby from the
open window having flown in from the garden and now
flittering its wings the way ladybugs do as if
shaking dust particles off of them and neatly arranging them
back under their hard red case

Midas poised his finger above her for one introspective moment
or perhaps out of a twinge of human hesitation then
ping! A golden ladybug hatpin or
doll's ornament encased in golden stasis

Pleased the king looked out the window at the
world its trees and palatial gardens so well-ordered so
clearly and royally geometrical and rubbed his fingertip on the

windowsill that immediately gleamed and
then on the window glass that suddenly became
opaque shutting out that pleasant vista

then tables and chairs and vases and knickknacks
given him by all the world's dignitaries and
already priceless until a

uniform kind of stainless steel glow of golden light shone
everywhere each detail of each item down to the
threads on a screw or the points on the royal pens

until King Midas had no recourse but to
touch himself as well the only one

so far left out of the equation

and he suddenly clunked to a complete and
formidable stop

his blood turned to gold in golden filigree veins
spread like coral throughout his solid body

heart chambers golden lungs golden skeleton a golden tree
his tongue heavily solid in a solid gold mouth

only his eyes remaining alive

seeing all this

9/29

29 VERY TINY GAZELLES

1

Very tiny gazelles crossing a tiny patch of sand
in the way they run and leap as if on springs

Also small elephants casting small shadows
on copper-colored earth on their way to
drink at a puddle

Then very small humans of famous Lilliputian size
only they're us as seen from a greater perspective that
might if closer up find ants huge rather than
minute

But now these humans in their miniscule size are perhaps
in a better relational percentage than previously or than
what passes for normal and everyday by our perspective
little humans blowing each other up in the mistaken
name of this ideology or that but in reality

very mite-like or even nit-like gnat-like and laughably
little

2

Caterpillars understand this shrunken perspective this
reductive poem

for they're perfectly contented with their size as they
flutter forward on their myriad feet seeing things in
their world in equally perfect proportion

And the Titans retired behind a mythic mountaintop more
vapor perhaps now than actual
bask and lounge and play chess and
bocce ball and go about their albeit
neglected way as erstwhile thundering giants occasionally

looking down at us ant people and smirking a bit
nostalgically for the good old days when they
wielded power and had influence over our
winding ways

Oh the heart breaks to know that in our
unkaleidoscopic vision of ourselves we can
treat others roughly unjustly blam through family
house-doors in full artillery in our search and seizures
thoroughly at ease with our size

taking it for granted and even feeling that
we'll be this perfect size forever as we

plow our presumptive way

10/2

30 HORSE KNOWLEDGE

"*Horse knowledge is one thing,*" said the horse doctor
bent over so much he's begun to resemble a horse

"*And you'd never confuse a whinny with an oratorio*"

"*But knowledge of God is a light emitted from
the rarest of shells discarded on the most
inaccessible of beaches*" said the rare shell collector
just back from the tropics with a full bag

"*And you'd never confuse a conch with a couch*"

"*I shall set sail in the morning against a scarlet sky*"
shouted the old salt gazing out at the salt sea
eyes already trained to distinguish a dot from something
like land or commotion out on the horizon's ocean

"*And go to the ends of the earth in search of the only thing
worthwhile searching for which can't be
quantified and remains aloof though our own
disappearance into its distant nearness is what is
to it most dear*" he continued stomping away on his
one Melvillian leg the other of diamond or wood
depending on his mood

And you wouldn't confuse the thump of his stump
with a postage stamp though on
down ramps he goes like a tank

*"The knowledge of one inch of space that actually
lights it from within even that is
beyond us"* said the firefly to itself as it
lit its way from one darkness to the next

And you wouldn't confuse its blink with a
blind alley nor its flickering flight with

gnosis

10/3

31 ANGEL PRANKS

1

A sober angel smites a laughing angel with a
horsehair feather and the laughing angel becomes a

sudden glass staircase each step of which is an
octave higher than the last

so someone ascending would soon be singing far beyond what
any planetary creature might hear

and only treetops in dense forests might notice the
sky singing in such gloriously watery tones

And the sober angel becomes a hill of rushing black
horses making huge dust clouds behind them and with
round black nostrils loudly snorting as they
charge the tripod on which is balanced one planet
indivisible under the sun or alongside the sun in its
elliptical orbit humming similar harmonies

Both angels then resume angelic form again and
fly off in opposite directions only to

meet again at the equator belt buckle almost
head on

2

One angel flies a locomotive through the sky
then lets it down carefully onto its tracks
way past midnight so all its passengers stay peacefully asleep

Another angel changes the direction of all the
houses on a hill but another angel changes
the directions of the hills as well so no one notices the
difference

A very dubious angel makes all Halloween costumes
real for a moment so that real ghosts and real
devils ring doorbells demanding sweets
but they snap back right away before too much
damage is inflicted
and his nature is under study to determine just how
angelic he is or whether he's in fact a mischievous djinn

Generally the pranks are more celestial and
nothing serious as in the case of the aurora borealis
suddenly parting like a movie theater curtain and
an angel on horseback taking the form of Tom Cruise
gallops across the sky

but before the beholders can make sure it
closes its shifting purplish draperies back to borealis again

But this is either bogus since angels can only do
what they're commanded or else
as proven by the high jinks of dolphins at sea
God's sense of humor sometimes does go overboard
such as the multitalented deepsea octopus that changes
color and texture to hide anywhere it wills
its body a kind of computer screen
where these intricate camouflage colors and textures
flicker into view then disappear
so an octopus with gray and ferny skin suddenly
materializes out of a gray rock of ferns for example
on a reef of bright orange coral and
scares the wits out of its intended victims

3

There's something that urges to burst out of
our boundaries in all this

that floats from inside ourselves or this
insubstantial idea of ourselves although corporeal

and floats equally everywhere outward to contiguous
extension with say watery landscapes or grassy
mountainsides the wind blows in all one direction

Somehow knowing we aren't these confined and
encapsulated persons born forever into only one
skin and destined to die unfulfilled in this

same too-tight flesh suit with its increasing
wear and tear affecting its actual workings

I see a glacial landscape in my mind's eye right
now of black shapes on dark blue water and
white clouds and blue-white ice and a
sky behind it that is uniformly a royal
light blue and I'm there as well as

hunched over a notebook page scribbling this down

Edges dissolve as heartbeats continue to prevail

Through which Allah creates the world

10/4-10/8

32 TERRIBLE

Terrible to knock on a door and
bats fly out

or bend to inhale the attar of rose
and get the smell of burning hair

to look at the stars and the whole
sky breaks open like a rotting melon

or kiss one's earthly beloved
and brush against a grin of skull-bone

What waves wash over us at dusk or dawn
that wear away the patinas of our usual
phenomenal expectations

Why should a cat not have wings and fly
or a fly have keys to a very swank automobile?

And why the wide river under the suspension bridge
not be purple with yellow-crested ripples in the
shapes of sunflowers?

Or the usual people we meet every day in passing
not suddenly show their radiant inner selves
like a procession of ignited creatures from angelic realms
but with their recognizable faces lighting up as
usual when they catch sight of ours?

At the threshold of the Next World there are giant causeways
guarded by compendia of sound in harmonious arrangements

And no matter how fast I write these poems
their melodies elude us

Every transformation continually takes place

What began as a fairly benign entity
will erupt its magma as red hot lava in a
nanosecond after sounding *"all's well"*

leading inevitably to a smooth unity of forms
but under vast miles of black pumice

and after the violent twister passes through town
uprooting houses like wool-tufts
an eerily beautiful dawn comes with its
sky-streaks of color and its various spotlights on
delicate arrangements of heirlooms and mementos

And a giant cowboy strides into town
and a dark stranger leaves an incomprehensible
message on a matchbook as he heads out the door at the
other end

This poem finds its beating heart and
loses it again on its way to
trumpet blasts of annunciatory clarity

the earth having turned through a number of
constellations and expanded imperceptibly to us

as we stand or sit or lie on it equally flexible
though radiantly corporeal after all

                                              10/11-16

33 RAMADAN RAPTURE

"They've taken our food away to the desert
they're feeding our food to the birds and the fishes
They've swiped all the food from our tables and kitchens
all the most scrumptious and delectable dishes

The fatted calves pigeon pies mincemeat in sauces
compotes and appetizers crudités and jams
Things done in nut butters things in puff pastry
aspics and tarjeens and sacrificed lambs

Oh what shall we do we'll go hungry we'll starve
without all those mainstays to our health and wellbeing
The candies and bonbons quince pies and peach melbas
each scrap and morsel now hurriedly fleeing

We'll be left sucking bones or our infantile thumbs
we'll sit on the floor and stare into space
We'll cry for our mummies and like mummies we'll grimace
all the color and glow will go out of our face"

So sings Desire in chorus with Appetite
thinking the world has gone lifeless and gray
For once in their lives they have to go hungry
from dawn to sunset for one month every day

Leaving our bodies at rest from their torments
our stomachs in shackles while the bright sun shines
To remember Who gave us each morsel and delicacy
set free for one month from our bodily confines

To die before death where the menu is meager
though in Paradise each goodie is multiplied in quantum
This world a pale shadow in comparison
O let's urge ourselves there with greater momentum!

34 THE POEMS I WANT TO READ

I have to write the poems I want to read

Of the green bicycle that flies through flames into a
crystal world with multiple windows like a fly's eyes for sky
and it's riderless so we can all ride on it to purest
safety after absolute daring with wheels spinning
and sparks flying from circumferences into the air
going out across the cable stretched from
building to building over a busy street or over a
canyon chasm whose rapids are even busier

And somehow smack in the middle having an original thought
or even losing the grip of thought altogether at such a
boundaryless altitude and on such a
flimsy vehicle to enter
God's mind of sweet amplitude in a direct ray of light
thinner than a sword blade slicing through a single hair
and the two halves falling away

The bicycle gets to the other side but not before
changing color and shape a multitude of times even
as many times as our breaths from birth outward
and it sees the distancing mountains recede with their
snow peaks and rainbow sunlight and news of the
near-naked hermit who lives there who's
abandoned everything we generally hold so dear

and who wraps great silvery feathered wings around him to
keep out the cold

which suspend him over valleys and more
populous cities as he seems to drift salt or
starlight behind him as he goes

as these poems also elude me

for it's not poems we want at all
it's breath and the perfect heartbeat

it's the note of certainty really that slides down the
tonic scale to our ears from somewhere
far beyond sound

to be taken and enwrapped

in pure sunlight especially here and now
in the middle of this thin
perpendicular night

2

To be the filament inside a light bulb
incandescent with beauty
and fully lit

Ah I wish these were my last utterances that
their poignancy be more acute

God's heartbeat hard against mine
in a physical encirclement that reaches
past even the most invisible galaxies

Alone with me here on an iceberg
melting faster than it does

to let the sheer splendor through

We're in a physical world that ticks all around us
yet move forward from side to side
as dolphins do
and cormorants and bounding deer

though we may not bound so prettily up a
rocky hillside past giant ferns bowing in a breeze

Love is the incessant heartbeat that
holds us together and the pulsing breeze
that enwraps all around us

though I seem to be writing on water

always just out of earshot

even my own earshot

And a gentle insistent thudding
beyond even my own heartbeat

3

The sky full of stars is where
splatter-drips have fallen where
ignited saints walked through the heavens and
out through the night

The stars are spear-pricks of warriors
inverted on the other side where their vast
light shines through

Dead children swimming up heaven their
luminous hearts beating ever-so-slightly

The stars talk across to each other
in grammatically correct twinkles

They're alive and dead celestial bodies in the
liquid suspension of space orbiting or
centrally burning or giving off last flames

The chug of divine vehicles across nothingness
on their way to the perfect appointment

Stars the internal organs of which we are the
eyes and ears and intergalactic silence the
mouth

Stars are punctuation of the holy sentence which
is coming to its conclusion and does so
within all of us turned inside-out at last
and all our elements drift finally free into space
whose central gravitational word is love

God's own special golden julep at the heart of it
His Word we ourselves speak when we listen to the roar
of quiet leaf-drift or the patience of a still spider at its
central pivot on its web

The word we ourselves speak on the tongue of The Real
lopsidedly symmetrical and perfectly flawed

not one singing atom not where it should be

not one star unknown to our innermost affections

10/26

35 THE RADIANCE OF DAY

The radiance of day is poured slowly into seven tall flasks
all a dark cobalt blue sitting on a past-midnight windowsill

A crane with its wings behind its back like a pacing barrister
walks back and forth in front of the misty lagoon of night

We've all been sent letters which need flame to unseal and
heat to decipher holding their invisible writing over our hearts

God's Majesty comes not from thunderclouds or cataracts
but from space itself we're enveloped in like infants by motherly arms

There's no end in sight for those whose hopes are eternal
and eternity like a walnut in its shell is creased and curled inside
each moment

We haven't arrived here in this hospitable place in vain
nor will we leave it at last without observing the proper formalities

Seven seas lying across from each other framed by continents
seven heavens of light and darkness leveled one on top of the other
all the way up all the way down

His bright light presiding perfectly over all
His warm deep darkness mending us through sorrow

One flower is enough to burst through human obscurity
One black rose of perfection turning to absolute silver then
ineffable quicksilver

Don't leave without your head or your hat and coat

Nobody can withstand at last the shearing wind of love

10/31

36 THE ROAD

There is a road that refuses to go any further
without reaching apotheosis and uttermost divine epiphany

It stops being horizontal and rises imperceptibly into its own light
not lifting bodily from its level but changing subatomically into finer stuff

It's determined and intent on not simply meandering forward
and though it is already faced in a definite direction
it still can go both ways both forward and back

Trees and lakes and adult-antlered stags peer out between conifers
astonished at the sudden transformation

Each pebble gleams each dirt-speck and grass blade between
dirt-specks bathed outwardly from somewhere far within
in uncanny splendor

A mouse drops its hard-won seed in astonishment
A bear reaches back from its honeycomb thievery and
scratches its head

The road furrows its brow in deeper concentration
sets its jaw and grits its nitty-gritty teeth

And the greatest wonder of it all is that whoever takes one
step on it is suddenly transported not forward nor upward
but southward non-geographically northward not by the
compass eastward and westward at once non-magnetically

and feels the supreme wind of light flow to each
outermost and innermost of their nonself-selves though the
road below them stays
steadfast as ever and though it rolls out before them as
normal yet there is no road left to go on but the
one road

not mere parable or metaphor
but the true embrace and the immoveable transportation

more a voice than a landscape

more a call now than a destination

more a reply within the call inside the voice
of the embrace

that brings light to the face

            10/31

37 THE WORLD'S BUNDLE / NOVEMBER 3, 2004

I'll put the bundle of the world entire on my back and

head windward away from its chill stillness

along the ridge road out past the edge

A whining dog might bring you
to your senses

Autumn trees casting the gold coins of their
leaves down at your feet in drifts
might show you real wealth

An icy wind that could slice your head from your
neck from behind in the name of
none but the change of seasons might show you
another's bitter truth

But know that lowering a bucket far down into the
dark well of the heart is required when
unjust bulwarks loom so menacingly against a
thundercloud sky

Passing one dead man suspended in a tree-crotch
then another and another over there among the
stubble-field's hay bales
can't deflect your main intention and its
carrying-out

to enter past the four elements and their
hybrids and nervous thoroughbreds

A ghostly presence at the doorway will only let you enter
into its ghostliness

so pass by that sound of squeaking hinges no matter
how inviting it may seem and don't let your
profile make an impression in its haunted wax for even
one particle of a second

but keep to the path
set out from within you

and so shall I

11/3

38 THE DEAD

The dead don't come back in the same form

It's we who might envisage them among the
misty cobalt tumblers catching a glimpse of

face or flicker of gesture

But they've gone on inert and free or free and
afloat through what is even tinier than a needle's eye
and more unmanageable than a camel

in the sense that it's totally out of our control now that
we're dead

All the hats that fit our heads and the socks we pulled on

All the clearings of throat for the next announcement
and the razor-sharp guilt cuts leaving their
telltale nicks

All and all again and all all over again now really
less than mist among the massively unremembered
stretching in their subterranean homes from
pole to pole and along either side of the equator

at attention with deeds

Their words sunk back down into their natal soil
thoughts drifted back out to circulate among stars

And the long shadowy trudge past the crest of the
hill and down the other side

into spectacular sunlight

11/4

39 THE SLEEP TRAIN

I'm in a hurry now to catch the next sleep train
because the last sleep train was just too slow

I've had two hours of sleep when I woke up suddenly
and I need a couple more before I wake up completely

I don't know what sleep is but dreams fly away with us
landing us in strange rooms with weird conversations

Only a few dreams survive the waking-up only a few squeak through
maybe the true dreams that are trying to tell us something

True dreams with their cast of characters sometimes from
heaven sometimes from hell and you often can't tell the difference

But our bodies know they need so much sleep or less
or so much more than we give them to run perfectly smoothly

The cat's at the foot of the bed undislodged for all my
tossing and turning snoring and dream-surfing dream colliding

The room is the same as I left it though I could be
Rip Van Winkle and look outside and it's two thousand fifty or more

The battery clock is still ticking though and I don't think
they've guaranteed it for fifty years and the cat's still purring

I can feel the sleep train slowing down now for me to hop on
and clear a way through night-clouds of steam and obstruction

to emerge again in a few hours refreshed and ebullient
arms and legs akimbo and almost ready for anything

11/8

40 TONGUE-TIP TO TONGUE-TIP

The mark of a good fruit may not be its
shape or its color but its taste

The tongue is a history of genealogical time all the way
back through mammal and reptile to the first gorgeous
round stones shiny as opals in primordial seas

Our eyes taste and our ears speak and our tongues are
dumb before God's glory in a gnat or butterfly
escaping through a window or pausing on a leaf or a
bear bumbling through brambles to the scent of sweetness

Flies look brutish as they gaze at their objective unknown to
us but kept firmly in the fly's mind until it reaches its destination

Everything sings in its own registers and makes
harmonies with the most unlikely of opposites
hard rock and feather lofty soul and burnt ember
burning house and spider in its web waiting for dinner

A passage is always made in the obdurate hillside
into which or out of which those clothed in splendor may climb
to safety

This poem is on its eighth stanza and still hasn't begun
my life is on its 64th year and I feel like a crawling infant
heading for its mother and calling out in the night

The ceilings are lower than before or the floors more elevated
the walls closer in and the doors narrower
but all roads lead to the same end

Even time ticks in our veins with each heartbeat
putting all the clocks to shame

Beauty glorifying itself in simplicity and
simplicity in beauty though our generalizations may pass
both of them over in favor of the destructive flame

If you pass yourself on the way back you'll know
what you never knew before you dared to
extend yourself out past the most daunting of shadows

Without trying to be wise or profound the simple apple
peeled or unpeeled yields its first and last sweetness with each
first and last bite of ours in the light of day
or the calm of twilight

If God is present everywhere then He is Present now
and if He's hidden He's nowhere to be found but
here in His magnificent Hiddenness as
widely forever as this moment is right now

If we sit still long enough it will all come to us
and if we get up to get it it will elude us and then fall
into our hands or hearts and
transform us into mice in fields of ripe wheat
on a summer's day in Idaho – Oh *I don't know…*

God sat with the dawn and taught it how to spread
to the farthest corners of the globe and over everyone
in equitable increments

He sat with the night and whispered deep secrets into its
black ears before setting the moon and planets into motion

Our tongues listen as they taste its dark sweetness
unable to comprehend in words what they know in pure sensation

tongue-tip to tongue-tip across this wide creation

                                            11/8

41 THE FOREST OF SLEEP

The forest of sleep opens onto a moonlit glade

The screw of waking is turned and the entire world is lit

Faces fall into place with idiosyncratic aplomb
each twisted or turned into benign or reactive expressions
especially the eyes which never lie

I would hold the heart high in the wind
to cleanse both heart and wind

The history of a moment dwindles into its manifestation
each of its hologram scenes sent by He-in-Whose-
Imagination-we-all-thrive

Who says *"Be!"* and without seduction or
nervousness besets what was there in original light
now clothed in materiality in order to submit
and finally apotheosis in death's light-time

Before we know it the entire world will be
in disarray
and its raw rough beauty exposed

Only the noble ones who hold onto the pearl
though it may not even be made yet in the oyster's vulva

its light brings peace to the strata we wish to destroy

11/10

42 I LAY BACK DOWN

I lay back down on my bed since I'd
only gotten five hours of sleep and as

soon as my head hit the pillow
a tall vertical light appeared and inside that light

my shaykh appeared smiling and inside his form
a space of green leafiness and Paradise sensations appeared

and inside that space an extension into unknown
regions appeared and that extension opened onto

a plain of light and swirling dunes and that
plain opened onto a heaven of stars and

inside that heaven a tunnel appeared filled with
blue flames incandescent with song and beyond that

incessant flickering a giant wingéd figure appeared
and within that figure a night appeared of eternal depth

and inside that night a void human form appeared
and that form was myself and the heart of that

self was every heart and every song sung on earth
and every inspiration beyond earth and

that was the gift to me which though I
didn't see these things the imagistic thought

came to me with great
intensity and I got back up and wrote it here

for all to see

11/12

43 A VERMIN'S TALE

A vermin wakes up to itself as a vermin among vermin
and pleads with the god of vermin to be
taken to a higher plane

Now for the purposes of this parable the god of vermin
is more than that for sure but the side facing vermin
at least according to the vermin themselves
is the one which
vermin recognize as their god

He grants vermin their sustenance their livelihood and
numerous vermin mates and vermin offspring
and except for poisons set out by the anti-vermin factions
life for a vermin is very good as it is for all other
creatures

But this vermin (I'm resisting naming him Herman)
really sees beyond his lot to a higher calling and then
sees himself rooting around in filth and offal and
sees himself on a mountain of light and somehow even
airborne like say the dragonfly

Hemmed about by the vermin world where being
vermin is the norm and one's parents and peers want you to
be a paragon among vermin but no more
our vermin hero wants to shake off his verminhood completely and
turn against his deepest vermin nature and go outside the
circle in which all vermin endlessly circulate

So he prays and begs and gets down on his six knees
antennae quivering and his little hard case vibrating with passion and
anguish
"Oh God of vermin surely You can do anything
so please make me anew as a new state of being completely
and I can leave my vermin past behind
transcend the garbage and be free"

There in a dusty corner of the shed in the one
ray of sunlight he can find
our vermin hero shakes and pleads shakes and prays

and the afternoon turns golden and mice run by
machinery is turned off for the day and
generators chug on for the night
and still our vermin hunkers down huddled in prayer

I'm not really sure how to have the god of
vermin answer his prayer or perhaps God keeps the
answer to Himself while somehow
comforting this humblest acolyte

The vermin's vision of a greater state alone might be a
kind of answer or perhaps the vermin's gnosis is in
knowing Who it is Who gave him that vision and so really
by that alone sees that he exceeds normal
verminity

A light maybe appears and maybe our vermin
not realizing the stages of its natural
progress the way wriggly maggots turn into flies

sprouts wings his hard case cracks and falls away
and he zooms off into daylight as glad as a born-again of
any creature relieved of its usual burdens

Or he could turn into a grown man with a vermin past

Or just become a truly enlightened vermin content to be
simply vermin as God created him now seeing his
rôle clearly in the cosmic pattern a submitted and contented vermin
through and through from feeler to flange-tip

Or I could say there's really no way of knowing
since it's not for us to communicate with the
vermin world except as destroyers and maybe our
thoughtless hand brushes him away one day or
crushes him with our shears

The enigma continues for all of us
but I'd like to think his prayer was answered by that
aspect of the god of vermin which is the entire greater
dimension that includes moose and market analysts and
meteors

And our vermin in perhaps a new shape completely is now
transformed and setting his sights on something
even greater

11/15

44 THE DYNASTY OF DURABILITY

The dynasty of durability has almost entirely expired
the dynasty of disappearance is descended upon us

Hooves raised and their shadows fallen across our faces
the unearthly rumble so audible it's almost edible

Yet both dynasties are finite and then another dimension or
dynamic or dignity dawns and that's the one I

want to be aligned with right now says the pelican
scooping up fish in its bill for later and wheeling

off into endurable daylight

"That's the one I inhale into my family tree in
hopes it guarantees some ultrasensory longevity in the

characteristically cosmic sense so

we might be truly inspired to inhale and exhale
with the angelic orders of the finches and the fish"

11/22

45 THERE'S THE TRAIN THAT STOPS

There's a train that stops at all the stops
and there's an express that doesn't stop but
shoots to the end

There's a woman in burlap who sells potatoes
her face a potato her feet in cardboard
but if you buy from her your roots distend and
your eyes grow parboiled

There's nothing wrong with lightning that strikes an abyss
unless it's filled with picnickers or runaway slaves banking on
freedom

The express train would take us all in safety
but not all of us are safe

For some the end of the line is at the beginning
and no matter how fast the train goes
the end is always near

For others each tree passed as it blurs past is
new and covered in furry light standing tall in its
singular sweetness from tip to root

The earth may not be flat as it falls off at the
sunset curve but its rondure turns imperceptibly to those who
walk its circuitous ways

God whispers into the captain's ears as the
night train chugs around curves

lighting the world with an uncanny brightness

11/24

46 ALCHEMICAL WEDDING

When it was time for the wedding
antlered stags surrounded the enraptured circle

Fir trees shed fine silvery needles that splintered the
first morning light as they filtered to the ground

A phoenix even looked all around with its fiery eyes
as it rose in a column of escalatoring flame

A chorus of crickets began their polyphonies across
canyons and fjords until the whole sky was clicking

The couple drew aside webbed shadows from their faces
until their eyes met and fresh amber oozed from the trees

Blips from the black pond resounded with the life both
around it and inside it from deep down fishy darkness
and deep-throated frog romances

The wedding of moisture and duration longevity and breath
so many rays of focused light beamed triangularly down from
openings in clouds to make golden the
arena of this alchemical celebration

Moose and killdeer oriole and poplar arrived as if newly born
from non-existent distances

The wedding of perception to reality and heartbeat to lung-beat
from the eye's pupil's depths to the vibratory
trembling that shudders from the center of everything

A beaker bubbles over as a fine hair meanderingly falls through light

A geode opens like a bud as a feather fans out into
a complete singing bird that flies away

We were all present and saw them exchange their holy vows in a
mirror of perpendicular black and white rainbows

Saw them as their faces were bathed in blue quicksilver

Are with them now in their most intimate solitude

Wake with them in their eyes after the latch-creak of
first morning light

The language they speak is forever uncorrupted

The song they sing is amazement's silent seashell
echoing back their own ears' listening

11/25

47 THE WAY OF THE WORLD

A rich man said to a poor man that
snow would be his wealth

A fireman said to a fire that he'd
encase the flames in ice

A sow bug said to her sow bug offspring
that one day they would all be butterflies

A fence said to the backyard it contained
that it was a rolling hillside full of sheep

Madame X looked deep into an old man's eyes and said
that one day he'd be a famous acrobat

A cat said the food better get better
though her owner thought she was
just meowing for a scratch

If the universe sang the whole truth for once to us
instead of in small leaps that revolutionize our
scientific understanding of ourselves

If only orthodoxy would be revealed all at once
like flat earth becoming round the sun becoming central
or the fact that all babies are the result of some kind of
sexual exchange

And all the other arcane secrets lurking today in
shadows we don't even realize are shadows

But maybe the laboratory is only half-lit even late at night
and the items we already know in spotlit splotches
are all we need know for now to accommodate our
unruly and often ruthless natures

Split atom knowledge having made Frankenstein
monsters of some of the best of men
wearing the ash of Hiroshima on their clothes
and leaving it in bad footprints across the
late night laboratory floor

If we sit upright we'll breathe

If we consult our hearts frequently we'll
see the light we need to see our
heart's unwavering celebration by

But as the world goes the
dust says to the tabletop *"Don't worry
I'll just be here for a moment"*

The fatal car accident says to the passengers inside it
*"Don't worry we'll just back up out of this and be
as good as new"*

And Death says to all of us
"I'm going fishing in other waters from now on"

It's the way of the world
that we can know only a tiny quivering
fraction of it before we go

It's the way of the Creator
that with love
we can know Him directly

          11/26

48 GRACE DESCENDING

The sound of water over rocks
is grace descending

The sound of animals in the distance
is the future coming toward us

The sound of light sliding over light
is God's Name being whispered to us

The sound of a door swinging open on its hinges
is our entrance into His Garden

There all sounds intermingle
water light songs hats shoes and roses

The sound of crackling flames
mortality's inner signaling

The sound of screeching brakes
the devil's near defeat

The sound of cries for help
the heart's compassionate response

The sound of knives being sharpened
the soul's anticipation of release

The sound of a baby's gurgles
God's angels happily memorizing

The sound of deer bounding away
our silent amazement at His perfection

A beloved voice in the dark
the sound of His near assistance

Our last sigh in this life
His cordial greeting

11/27

49 THE LION WHO WANTED TO SING

There once was a lion who wanted to sing

I don't mean he wanted to roar better than the
other young adult lions following in their
furry forefathers' paw-steps standing in

silhouette on crags terrorizing the other jungle
denizens by lifting his hairy jowls in loud throaty literal caterwauls

This lion perhaps had passed by a hunter's camp and overheard
opera on the crackling camp wireless while the
hunters were whiskying themselves up for the kill
and he stopped and cocked his ears to catch
the subtle strains of Verdi or Puccini or even (Lord help us) Wagner
and his heart opened to the strains of very unlionlike
singing

Ungravelly unthroaty unfrightening glorious aria-belting
song

But as a lion he found himself in a very strange pickle
often trying out a few sweet little buzzes as he slid through
tall grasses toward buffalo herds distracted by inner
strains of Italian music

At first he only trembled his lips as he tried to
raise his natural range more liltingly
but only wheezed and seemed to whimper

Cranes honked by monkeys chattered and screamed
peacocks cried their high dry cackle but nobody
he could learn from in the animal kingdom
quite sang like Renata Tibaldi Lauritz Melchior or Pavarotti
and he padded along somewhat hopeful and
generally heartbroken the way late teenagers on the
cusp of adulthood generally feel

When no one was paying him any particular
attention he sought out some other folk for
cantorial advice
approaching the hippopotamuses for example
lying around in the
mud their noses above muck-level though when they
caught sight of him they generally submerged
or headed away down the river tails twirling and his
pleas sounded like more lion subterfuge than a
cry for vocal advice and anyway hippos are hardly the
best advisors in this matter judging from their song though their
mouth-spread is operatic but our lion was
young and experimental

At midday when the others were flat out asleep
he would go off from the pride and try out a
few melodious notes but he only ended up lightly
roaring in a slightly higher register and
so lay with head on paws distraught with
even a few tears in his eyes and in his
brain that glorious wireless sound soaring above the baobabs
with its occasional static crackle and
whistly squeaks

2

And so the years went by

and our young lion grew older and stranger
as many of us do

never finding an adequate voice coach to
coax him out of what grew progressively
coarse and less like meowing and more like
roaring

Here he is with full mane and that lengthy slouch so
perfected by male lions
except that he's pretty much been ostracized by the
other lions and lives as a loner uninterested in
the hunt or fighting for supremacy and a
harem of lissome and lithe she-lions
but rather prowls around with tunes in his
shaggy head listening for a pure song out of a

stork or a phalange of flamingos or even a
gazelle or giraffe (having heard that the
giraffes' silence is a myth and that they *do* make
high-pitched sounds he waits appreciatively at the
edge of a giraffe enclave but they're so
petrified to see him they've gone completely mute after all)

Elephants make almost singing sounds especially
basso profundo whale-groans heard by

other elephants even miles away but they proved to be
unfriendly tutors whenever somehow he made his
presence rather than his absence known
they'd prick up those giant windmill-blade ears of theirs
and pounce around in his direction and
scare off our feline Don Quixote for good

Then one day an Italian Count went safari-ing
blunderbuss in hand and wandered away from his
party on some dreamy hunch or other and found himself
lost

In a panic he did what he always did when scared but never
before in thick pampas grass in a Kenyan jungle
he sang arias in a high clear tenor from a
veritable potpourri of Italian operas

Our lion happened to be napping
but came suddenly awake in what he
at first mistook for having died and gone to heaven

His prayers were answered!
An angel was approaching!
His voice coach to teach him to reach new
vocal heights *had arrived!*

He went toward the singing and found the
Count sitting in a sweat on a rock blunderbuss at his side
so he stealthily slunk close to the ground
and cautiously approached

The Count was sitting with eyes closed tight and glottis
vibrating like an earthquake
Puccini Rossini Verdi then Puccini and Rossini again
then more Puccini

The lion plucked up some courage and tried a few
harmonies from his low vantage

The Count stopped suddenly and blinked open his eyes
thinking he too had perhaps lapsed into a
coma and died and been transported to
another less material realm

When the rest of his party finally found him
(and though this is entirely made up I want to say
"I kid you not") they discovered

the Count on his rock singing his heart out
and the lion at his feet singing in close harmony with him
caroling and spiraling up through the atmosphere in
clear melismatic melodies
two tenors in perfect sync

Happy lion and delirious Count and
astonished courtiers all unfortunately with their
own artillery so that this

story may end badly but for the
image of man and beast singing opera together in some
jungle somewhere
and the lion's happy fulfillment so that

really he doesn't care if he lives or dies now
and in fact has *really* died and gone to heaven in his
big operatic lion heart

so unbelievably happy is he

3

Though in fact our lion probably yowled and
growled and roared the way young lions must
but in its reluctance to pounce the Count
heard melodious opera sweet as a living reprieve to his ears

And if a lion were to appear in my bedroom right now
I'd be awed by its majestic beauty and
scared to death to move a single muscle even one twitch or two

sitting still as a rock in hopes the lion would be bored enough
to finally get up slink up the stairs and slide out into the
neighborhood (where there are
lots of juicy teenagers!)

But if it sat and sat with its wonderful MGM
head framed by my lamplight and just straight-ahead
looked at me with some inscrutable beastly
decision circulating round in its head

I might come to consider it reciting gorgeous epic poetry by its
wheezes and low gutturals and unflappable heroic composure its

perfectly leonine kingliness full of hair-raising battleground secrets
or even lyric poetry of a particularly jungly surrealist kind maybe
snatches of Aimé Césaire or verbal descriptions of the paintings of
Henri Rousseau (the possible model for this bizarre rendezvous)

And if it let me alone (though I know cats love to
toy with their food before dining) I'd imagine
all sorts of scenarios of lionesque perfection in which
even singing opera might be included or even better considering its
natural animal magnetism and majesty
delivering a learned discourse in High Theology and
ultimate pure dissolution of the animal self in God

so relieved I'd be not to be immediately eaten

As we all are with that
great lion haunch always sitting not far off from us
gazing far off somewhere while still aware of our subtlest
movements our subtlest changes from state to state

even our subtlest thoughts

just beyond the little circle of lamplight in which we live
paws out in front of it and its flanks curled languorously under it and
that ponderous paintbrush tail occasionally
thumping the ground with its poignant burst of impatience

But above all the absolutely leonine face of the lion its
benign ferocity beauteously coiled up within it and those
straight-ahead staring topaz eyes of his

and those unforgiving teeth sharper than death
through which melodiously whistles its operatic breath

Arias of love and death one after another
with each breath

One continuous aria after another
of love and death

                              12/7

50 MORE SUNLIGHT LET THROUGH

No matter how many multicolored flowers in vases
or how many roses explode from their bushes
long after their season is over

or how many antelope stand to beautify the
margins of our existence before bounding away

or how many thick slates are taken away from between
us and the sun in order to let in more light

the lips in our lips to sing praises and show actual gratitude
are too numb or silent though our lips themselves
might form the usual sentences or sing the usual songs

It's the lips in our lips and the gesture deep
within gesture and something at the core of the
words we employ like classical masks that
steps out from behind them all with
radiant gesture and a word or two that

actually brings forth equally radiant children from their
dark molecules who perpetuate word and gesture
even long after we're gone

The heart of the matter that sets flowers in
vases in the let-through sunlight and adds

perfect roses picked at their perfect prime
at just the right time that changes

gratitude into our innermost body shuddering to
the surface of our physical one becoming
one with it that animates us completely

and then changes the world around us
oh I don't know

into more antelope at the margins bounding away

or more slates taken away and more

sunlight let through

                                              12/8

51 DIRECT PASSAGE

Doesn't anyone know what is really going on
inside us but God?
Is He the only One?

There's a silent wall of golden plumaged birds
ascending vertically into a topaz blue sky

At the top of the world is a radiant white disk
turning slowly through the spectrum casting its
colors on all creation

Do we even ourselves really know what is
going on inside us
or only God?

A mouse crosses a few boards above the drop ceiling in
search of crumbs and we hear its pitty-pat patter
below scurrying faster than thought

Windows in Venice go up on a glorious day of sunlight and
clouds reflected below in the canal's dark waters

If we go out into this world with eager emptiness to
see its wonders won't we see God? But if it's

only God Who knows us and no one else and maybe not
even ourselves after all

then what's to keep trees from igniting like torches or
cascades to be strands of music or lines of words
from tumbling into chaos and out again in exact grammatical
order?

The deeper we go inside do we see God
or do we see with God's eyes?

Or does He alone see us in our blindness
and is His
seeing then *our* seeing?

An elephant stood for a long time swaying
back and forth and then sat down
spraying his back with dust in perfect
humility

Giving up everything about ourselves we hold most dear
is certainly no loss in the long run and gains us
the light of eternity after all

A tiny dog feather flutters in the airshaft between
anterior intentions and later regrets

Something's always missing but it's never
anything real

If no one really knows us outside of ourselves but through a
makeshift amalgam of phenomenological puzzle-pieces
that make up our physical and reactive characteristics

and in our own darkness we only catch glimpses of
ourselves in passing or in sinking deeply into
Joseph's well until we're enslaved and
brought to Egypt

is it only God who can release us into
clarity? Dream interpretations intact?

*(Three disks of light over Kansas
first in triangular pattern and then their
separate ways to distant points in the
night sky)*

O Allah we sit in peaceful yearning

Let Your bright boat bestow on us
the swiftness of direct passage

to Your Presence

12/11

52 THERE WAS A REPLY

There was a reply over the fence but
nobody heard it

It was in our language
it had the grammar of saints and the radiance of sunlight

Some were plowing some were burying some woke up
to find their wealth gone and their health going

It was the reply we'd been waiting for and all our
heartbeats now audible here attest to our disappointment

It was as if water was poured over us but
no one got wet

All our questions formulated as questions but even
more all unspoken ones even ones in the
form of statements but that unknown to us
expected a reply

We wondered if somehow at least one of us
heard some of it so we could piece together a
coherent sentence

Everyone was asked *if* they heard or *what* they heard
and it was a strange brew after all

Crows nested in some of the things people said

Warriors defended their lives on blood-soaked battlefields

Ghosts took on rosy color and passed among us as
the living

Animals returned to their places usurped by humans
and fought and multiplied as before

Wastelands came back to life in a
moonlight of poppies

Fields so fertile they didn't need cultivating to
yield their nutritious riches
grew dark and fallow in the blink of an eye

With all eyes on the lame child who couldn't speak
who seems to have heard the reply complete
who knows what was said having heard it clearly
who would love to tell us but has no
words to tell us except with his eyes

We resumed our labors
we went on as before

some of us died without knowing
though none of us doubted a reply had come
and that our lives would be transformed and
ushered in to the Divine Presence to dwell there
forevermore if only we knew it

The newborn grew up knowing about it and
wishing someone would come forward to tell it

Did it fall on stones and streams
but they kept sitting still or running endlessly forward?

It's true our lives changed just by knowing it had come

Nothing was unaffected nor remained as it was

Everyone listened harder than ever to everything they heard
and even things they barely heard

It's said God appeared to the one who heard it
as he was about to die
which accounts for his youthful appearance in his grave
and the smile on his face

Or was it his lips forming the sentence after all
the yearned-for reply

and we each leaning down as close as
possible to those lips

to hear it?

12/20

53 A SHORT SHOE SAGA

The little shoe disturbed the universe with a single kick
though it brought nothing low nor disassembled the
delicate armatures

It had a pointed toe within which no toes lay
though "lay" isn't the right word exactly to describe
an absence of toes where toes should be

This shoe traveled through a great arc starting
somewhere near the North Star and ending with its
sore point of contact somewhere at the base of
our shins

It wore a grin as it hit and then continued hitting until it
made a complete circle and every soul of us
was somehow shoehorned within it

Sad shoe spinster shoe shoeless shoe

Plants grew out of it tenements grew up in it
it grew congested with squatters including
pigeons and retired locomotives

It goes on though day after day and night after night
tramping down a lonely road into sunsets
kicking the ground and
leaving its hideous mark its distinctive waffle
tread

In Siam it's a boot in Australia it's barefoot
in Moscow it's a stylish dress shoe in rainforests it
stands for a moment in mud before
plodding on

It has a tongue and eyes and laces itself up for
formal occasions

The second shoe never drops

That one's on its own

12/22

54 DOORS

Behind the black door of death cooked oranges or the
real thing

Behind the crystal door of light those two eyes that
see everything

Behind the endless corridor of this world those elusive shadows
running before us

Behind the door of flame the exact shape of our shape we must
go through a few relics we can rely on

for the flames can't touch us where the
world of love resides

Through the door of sumptuous gardens the
gnomes of Paradise

Behind the inner door inside the door we've gone
through a mist parts and a sound silences
a light presents a new face and a
roar becomes a pure conflagration

Words become inhabited by the weight of their meaning
each one a planet with its slow-revolving
moons

Statements are passed down a long hall
and when they finally reach us
they're a unique species of tropical parrot that
flies away in a fan of color

None of these doors or corridors exist even
those that open and close with their
knobs and keyholes slats and thicknesses

But get locked out of an impregnable house in
an icy wind with no way in and we see
what doors can be

And when the hinges start to sing in oiled harmonies
and obstacles melt the doors become openings
through which the white deer of solitude strides
holding up its head draped in
celestial roses its enormous eyes
translucent in the light
each one of its paces our heartbeats
that pulse us on

12/28

55 THE ALCHEMIST'S LESSON

The alchemist announced to his students
"Today we will transform death"

and they all looked at each other and gulped

But a bird in a cage sang three exquisite notes
and a salamander near an open fire turned to
copper

Three bouncing balls in a pewter bowl
swiveled to the rhythm of inaudible music

*"We shall transcend the material by attending to
the material in a way our preoccupied minds
never do"*

Then he flourished a rose and held it in the air
until it burst into flames
lighting the dark corners of the laboratory where
he and his twelve students stood

The flame-licks changed places with each other
and sang God's praises in their incessant
snap and crackle

One student fainted and had to be revived by
a collective focus of concentrated starlight

One student started singing an as yet untransmitted
sacred text in perfect melody

But the pain in my left shoulder hasn't really
subsided yet with this little exercise at 3:45 AM
(*sleepless so far tossing and turning until this moment*)

in that faraway lab in time and space where
the students look at their teacher with
perfect trust and he proceeds to the

alembics and flasks and produces out of his
breast pocket a heart-shaped object that
even pulsates in space

"*This*" he says to them "*is not alive and not
dead
it simply is
from birth to death*"

Then it suddenly expands until it is

the lab in which they stand and the bewildered students
as well and the teacher holding it between
forefinger and thumb and even

me with my shoulder pain and sleeplessness
and the cat purring next to me now and all the
tragedy in the world and all its origins

in our hearts fearing death unless it
happens to someone else which it

always seems to do

until that moment when we ourselves are

fanned by the void of their ventricles

and transformed into gold

12/31

56 LINE FROM A DREAM POEM

Time cannot fill all its minutes

1/1/05

57 SAGA OF THE SEA SPONGE

A sea sponge looked up through the water at the moon
*"Why am I trapped down here when I could be
basking in its glow? Schools of fish
obstruct me from a clear view
sea-murk obfuscates* (it was an
educated sponge)
*All I can do is cling to this rock or float
to and fro*

Peel back the ocean from our eyes to see the
moonlight direct

A longing for that vision might be enough to bring us near

Who dances in the moonlight but the moon's own
liberated rays?

And when day comes and the moon disappears
the clear view becomes a sudden absorption
in its single Source of light

Our hearts are made for that

They beat to find that wellspring then
go deep

Each beat's a heart-search
for reflection's Glorious Source

past day and its body of water down through whose
layers of currents that jug pours its pure
milk gallon on gallon to the sea sponge
meandering in its eyes
hoping for luck

When God is the only luck we'll ever have
to see Him clearly

1/1

58 WHY THERE ARE STARS

There's an alligator that opens its mouth
and everything else becomes silent

There's always something greater that engulfs
what is great

No roar so loud a louder roar won't
outroar it

No tyrant who won't look small one day
in his socks in a corner of the prison yard

No great trauma with its red eyes and flaring
nostrils that won't withdraw in quiet servitude

No great tragedy that won't be a scene of
singing birds and tentative crickets exploring

But meanwhile heavy boulders rain on our
paths and heads and bounce like
rubber balls

We can squint to see they are pebbles but
non-squinters will still get squashed

Seeing a rose where an abyss is won't
make it a rose though it look like
red petals on a stem

But I insist the juggling fool who sees visions
outwits the anguished Crusader questioning
staked witches and the dead

A sure heart in the desert has the strength to drink
water from a mirage

A blind horse may still reach his destination
with a backward rider and his tail in flames

Destinations will press close against us
when we fully face in their direction

Opening our hands and letting the world roll out
is the cure for both ourselves and the
world after all

When we let the world go it rises with its
natural buoyancy

It's not ours to keep
but only ours to release

The black sky fills with its glorious
scattered lights

1/6

59 THE SLEEP OF THE DEAD

must be a sweet sleep

So many do it

1/10

60 BUT IT IS WE

A ship is laden with pearls each one
previously strung and it's going to dock
in your harbor and they're yours
What will you do?

A face is waiting to be kissed that belongs to
someone you've not yet met who knows you from
head to toe who will lead you down the
mountain to safety
Will you follow?

The sky is moving closer to you by ultra-dimensional
increments with all its celestially roaring sounds
and all you need do is take one step to
be totally transformed
How will you respond?

These and several other miraculous cataclysms
are taking place each moment under our
gaze and under our fingertips and inside the
accordion music of our heartbeats on a
rainy side street in Paris where no feet
completely touch the ground and the
heady drink is perfectly admissible starlight

The grateful watch floodwaters rise and are
amazed

The ungrateful live in a universe the exact size of their
last suit of clothes complaining of their tight fit
and each speck of lint

Swan lands are always sailing into view

Welcoming signals are always being waved to us by their
friendly inhabitants with no ulterior motives but generosity
from very nearby

God has set the table with hundreds of
personal touches and will be
our attentive Help as we order
unfamiliar dishes for the first time

But it is we who will taste them

1/12

61 POEM GIVEN IN A DREAM

We will be brought before our Lord

like washing hanging on a line

1/18

62 LAST WILL & TESTAMENT

He sits down to write his Last Will & Testament
and a chorus of lost birds begins singing
all his favorite songs from childhood on

The yard around his house bursts into flame
and the yellow green halos flicker pictures from his
lost childhood

"I shall leave them India and China" he thinks to himself
as he writes down his paltry acre
*"and Samarkand and the crown jewels with the
Koh-I-Noor diamond surrounded by seed pearls"*
as he writes down the one railroad watch
handed down from his great uncle

Not every day does the light fall into the canyon this way
illuminating its rocks as if they were the
jeweled thrones of kings

Nor does it spangle the river like sparkler strands of
goddess-like hair to remind him of the
One God Who speaks to him through light-sight and
water-sound
as his memory scatters drops onto his
page one item at a time

*"The horse which is a house the coach which is a couch the
cat which is a coat the livery which is the mice in the walls*

*the proclamations and edicts which are the
scribbled notebooks of my years here before the
continual avalanche of wilted roses and beckoning owl-hoots"*

Even the silence is not his to give
yet he bequeaths it as well since it has
lately been in such short supply

A silence where you can almost hear
God's footsteps as He goes on His rounds
between mortals who need His care and
the ferns and dragonflies that float so
freely in His air

He sits over the blank sheet of his Last
Will & Testament where a trail of ants has
begun its wiggly trek carrying some of its
dead in miniscule jaws and a
procession of eggs like luminous rice grains held in
motherly mandibles

Not every day does darkness fill the
house with such lively bliss and seem to
outline each thing with a
discernable rainbow

He sees himself out the corner of his eye
taking sugar cubes to the horse in the lower
pasture as night comes on

He sees himself horizontally navigating this
rotating earth to the sea and then
out to the stars

and smiles to himself
even a smile that's not

completely his own

1/20

63 POEM THAT PUTS INTO PERSPECTIVE

I look down at my body in the hot bath
and see it's the body of a frog

Round white belly legs sticking out
well at least it's not the body of a dog

                                                                                     1/24

ABOUT THE AUTHOR

Born in 1940 in Oakland, California, Daniel Abdal-Hayy Moore's first book of poems, *Dawn Visions*, was published by Lawrence Ferlinghetti of City Lights Books, San Francisco, in 1964, and the second in 1972, *Burnt Heart/Ode to the War Dead*. He created and directed *The Floating Lotus Magic Opera Company* in Berkeley, California in the late 60s, and presented two major productions, *The Walls Are Running Blood*, and *Bliss Apocalypse*. He became a Sufi Muslim in 1970, performed the Hajj in 1972, and lived and traveled throughout Morocco, Spain, Algeria and Nigeria, landing in California and publishing *The Desert is the Only Way Out*, and *Chronicles of Akhira* in the early 80s (Zilzal Press). Residing in Philadelphia since 1990, in 1996 he published *The Ramadan Sonnets* (Jusoor/City Lights), and in 2002, *The Blind Beekeeper* (Jusoor/Syracuse University Press). He has been the major editor for a number of works, including *The Burdah* of Shaykh Busiri, translated by Shaykh Hamza Yusuf, and the poetry of Palestinian poet, Mahmoud Darwish, translated by Munir Akash. He is also widely published on the worldwide web: *The American Muslim, DeenPort*, and his own website, among others: www.danielmoorepoetry.com. The Ecstatic Exchange Series is bringing out the extensive body of his works of poetry, beginning in 2005 with *Mars & Beyond, Laughing Buddha Weeping Sufi, Salt Prayers* and a revised edition of *Ramadan Sonnets*, and continuing in 2006 with *Psalms for the Brokenhearted, I Imagine a Lion, Coattails of the Saint, Love is a Letter Burning in a High Wind*, and *Abdallah Jones and the Disappearing-Dust Caper*. In 2007, *The Flame of Transformation Turns to Light, Underwater Galaxies, The Music Space* and *Cooked Oranges* have continued his publication project.

POETIC WORKS BY DANIEL ABDAL-HAYY MOORE

Published and Unpublished
(many to appear in The Ecstatic Exchange Series)

Dawn Visions (published by City Lights, 1964)
Burnt Heart/Ode to the War Dead (published by City Lights, 1972)
This Body of Black Light Gone Through the Diamond (printed by Fred Stone, Cambridge, Mass,1965)
On The Streets at Night Alone (1965?)
All Hail the Surgical Lamp (1967)
States of Amazement (1970)

Abdallah Jones and the Disappearing-Dust Caper (published by The Ecstatic Exchange/ Crescent Series, 2006)
The Chronicles of Akhira (1981) (published by Zilzal Press with Typoglyphs by Karl Kempton, 1986)
Mouloud (1984) (A Zilzal Press chapbook, 1995)
Man is the Crown of Creation (1984)
The Look of the Lion (The Parabolas of Sight) (1984)
The Desert is the Only Way Out (completed 4/21/84) (Zilzal Press chapbook, 1985)
Atomic Dance (1984) (am here books, 1988)
Outlandish Tales (1984)
Awake as Never Before (12/26/84) (Zilzal Press chapbook, 1993)
Glorious Intervals (1/1/85) (Zilzal Press chapbook, ?)
Long Days on Earth/Book I (1/28 – 8/30/85)
Long Days on Earth/Book II (Hayy Ibn Yaqzan)
Long Days on Earth/Book III (1/22/86)
Long Days on Earth/Book IV (1986)
The Ramadan Sonnets (Long Days on Earth/Book V) (5/9 – 6/11/86) (Published by Jusoor/City Lights Books, 1996) (Republished as Ramadan Sonnets by The Ecstatic Exchange, 2005)
Long Days on Earth/Book VI (6-8/30/86)
Holograms (9/4/86 – 3/26/87)
History of the World (The Epic of Man's Survival) (4/7 – 6/18/87)
Exploratory Odes (6/25 – 10/18/87)
The Man at the End of the World (11/11 – 12/10/87)
The Perfect Orchestra (3/30 – 7/25/88)
Fed from Underground Springs (7/30 – 11/23/88)
Ideas of the Heart (11/27/88 – 5/5/89) New Poems (scattered poems, out of series, from 3/24 – 8/9/89)
Facing Mecca (5/16 – 11/11/89)
A Maddening Disregard for the Passage of Time (11/17/89 – 5/20/90)
The Heart Falls in Love with Visions of Perfection (6/15/90 – 6/2/91)

Like When You Wave at a Train and the Train Hoots Back at You (Farid's Book) (6/11 – 7/26/91)
Orpheus Meets Morpheus (8/1/91– 3/14/92)
The Puzzle (3/21/92 – 8/17/93)
The Greater Vehicle (10/17/93 – 4/30/94)
A Hundred Little 3-D Pictures (5/14/94 – 9/11/95)
The Angel Broadcast (9/29 – 12/17/95)
Mecca/Medina Time-Warp (12/19/95 – 1/6/96) (Published as a Zilzal Press chapbook, 1996)
Miracle Songs for the Millennium (1/20 – 10/16/96)
The Blind Beekeeper (11/15/96 – 5/30/97) (Published 2002 by Jusoor/Syracuse University Press)
Chants for the Beauty Feast (6/3 – 10/28/97)
Open Doors (10/29/97 – 5/23/98)
Salt Prayers (5/29 – 10/24/98) (Published by The Ecstatic Exchange, 2005)
Some (10/25/98 – 4/25/99)
Flight to Egypt (5/1 – 5/16/99)
I Imagine a Lion (5/21 – 11/15/99)(Published by The Ecstatic Exchange, 2006)
Millennial Prognostications (11/25/99 – 2/2/2000)
The Book of Infinite Beauty (2/4 – 10/8/2000)
Blood Songs (10/9/2000 – 4/3/2001)
The Music Space (4/10 – 9/16/2001) (Published by The Ecstatic Exchange, 2007)
Where Death Goes (9/20/2001 – 5/1/2002)
The Flame of Transformation Turns to Light (99 Ghazals Written in English) (5/14 – 8/21/2002) (Published by The Ecstatic Exchange, 2007)
Through Rose-Colored Glasses (7/22/2002 – 1/15/2003)
Psalms for the Broken-Hearted (1/22 – 5/25/2003) (Published by The Ecstatic Exchange, 2006)
Hoopoe's Argument (5/27 – 9/18/03)
Love is a Letter Burning in a High Wind (9/21 – 11/6/2003) (Published by The Ecstatic Exchange, 2006)
Laughing Buddha/Weeping Sufi (11/7/2003 – 1/10/2004) (Published by The Ecstatic Exchange, 2005)
Mars and Beyond (1/20 – 3/29/2004) (Published by The Ecstatic Exchange, 2005)
Underwater Galaxies (4/5 – 7/21/2004) (Published by The Ecstatic Exchange, 2007)
Cooked Oranges (7/23/2004 – 1/24/2005)
Holiday from the Perfect Crime (1/25 – 6/11/2005)
Stories Too Fiery to Sing Too Watery to Whisper (6/13 – 10/24/2005)
Coattails of the Saint (10/26/2005 – 5/10/2006) (Published by The Ecstatic Exchange, 2006)
In the Realm of Neither (5/14/2006 – 11/12/06)
Invention of the Wheel (11/13/06 – 6/10/07)
The Sound of Geese Over the House (6/15 –)

www.ingramcontent.com/pod-product-compliance
Lightning Source LLC
Chambersburg PA
CBHW020901090426
42736CB00008B/460